DOMINIC GARNETT

First paperback edition printed 2015. A catalogue record for this book is available from the British Library.

ISBN 978-0-9931204-1-1

Published by DG Fishing (for more copies of this book go to www.dgfishing.co.uk)

Designed and set by Garrett Fallon, Fisherman Creative Ltd

Printed in Estonia by Tallin Book Printers: www.trt.ee

Cover and internal illustrations by Lord Bunn (www.lordbunn.com)

Contents:

Introduction

I HAD IT ALL WORKED OUT. You know, that lukewarm two pages or so the author is supposed to start a book with that nobody actually reads. But sod that. I know I'm supposed to thank the organ grinder for the peanuts and say what a pleasure and a success it has all been. But the truth of it is more… crooked?

I am indeed extremely thankful for all the brilliant people in the fishing world who have given me friendship and support. Many of these stories are for and about them. But I've also had to kick as hard as a carp hooked in the arse for much of the work you now have in your hands.

So no, this isn't the standard introduction and this isn't the standard fishing book. This is warts, flies and all. This is that dodgy-looking swim you couldn't quite resist. This is blind hope and a spinner stuck in a tree. This is Norbert Darby's tenth blank and 100,000th roll-up cigarette. This is a set of bad directions to a river that took forever to find.

This isn't the River Test, but a towpath or that hooky little stream by the graveyard. This is the camaraderie of the bankside, crap cider and mosquito bites. This is misplaced hope and sudden drama. Blood, ink and the strange things that swim in Torquay Harbour. Hidden within these pages is the story of my fishing life. The best, the worst and the weirdest of it, anyway. And I mean every damned word.

It's not always easy to take the forked road in the fishing world, however. There is a certain protocol to follow with the articles you see season after season, that tend to involve a big fish, a grinning bloke, some tackle promotion and prose as flat as Norfolk. Nobody blanks, few risks are taken and all the smaller places and grubby details are missing. Much of the time though, editors are wary when you throw them a curve ball. Hence many of the pieces in this collection are the "ones that got away," if you like. So besides totally new work and one or two favourites, you'll also find the bits that were cropped, sanitised or rejected because they didn't fit the straightjacket of the commercial fishing article. So here they are with space to breathe, free and uncensored for the first time.

Perhaps the only slight disappointment were one or two crazier stories that were lost at the net. But such is fishing and not every mystery is solved or makes a tidy article. One classic "if only" was a pair of local nutters tackling a deep, weedy lake for a big catfish that had been attacking moorhens. They had taken to prebaiting with roadkill and launching dead squirrels into the depths. Sadly, nothing ever materialised and as I type this I wonder if they're still sat there waiting.

That's the thing about wild plans though; they don't always lead to wild results. If they did I might be a celebrated author, rather than a skint bloke with a garage full of random fishing tackle. But I'm still at it, fishing and writing. For now though, it's time for me to shut up and let you enjoy the stories in this book. So go ahead, lift the lid carefully and let them crawl out.

Dominic Garnett, 2015

Acknowledgements: I have many friends in the fishing world to whom I am eternally grateful for and they know who they are. Trying to make a living as an angling writer can be a thankless task and on more than one occasion I have felt like giving up entirely, if only for my own sanity. Some folks deserve a particular mention for keeping my chin up, providing an arm round the shoulder or a kick up the arse as and when required. Special thanks go to: Garrett Fallon, editor of the brilliant fishing quarterly *Fallon's Angler,* without whom this book would not have been possible. Paulina Mroczynska and all the Garnett family for their unwavering support. Merlin Unwin and Karen. Steve Partner, who might take the piss out of my beard, but has always backed me. Neil Bunn, for injecting your style and creativity into this project. Alex Garnett, for your keen eye and visual skills. Mark Bowler at Fly Fishing & Fly Tying. Simon Jefferies and all at Turrall. Stephen Stones. Kev Wilmot at Angling Times. Dr Mark Everard, Geir Sivertzen, Aidan Curran, Chris Lambert, Ian Nadin, Norbert Darby, Leon Guthrie, Russ Hilton, Jeff Hatt, Steve Roberts and all my other fishing friends for keeping me smiling and tempering my lows with so many highs.

Additional image credits, with many thanks: Simon Steer (p36-38), Ben Garnett (P42&108), Ron P Swegman/ Urban Angler Fly Shop NYC (p53&55), Ian Sheridan (p54), Chris Lambert (P69) Frazer McBain (P70, 78-83), Russ Hilton (p107), Andrew Pym (130-134)

Foreword
by Matt Hayes

THE ANGLING WORLD IS A MUCH-CHANGED PLACE FROM THE ONE I JOINED AS A BOY BACK IN THE 1960S. Tackle, clearly, is improved. Bait likewise and if carp are your bag, the choice has never been greater. But not everything has moved forward for the better. Like fishing writing.

Where once angling journals indulged the rich talents of Clive Gammon (my personal favourite), Richard Walker and Trevor Housby to name but a few, today's crop—bar the odd exception—seem to be commercially-driven robots lacking the wit, inclination or ability to do anything other than churn out product-laden dross that serves sponsors rather than readers.

Frankly, as far as fishing journalism goes, it's a pretty sorry state of affairs. But, as I said, there are some notable exceptions. Dom Garnett is one of them. While Dom shows a burning passion for fishing, he

"I enjoyed his irreverent, quirky and fresh style, his ability to paint vivid pictures and take his readers on journeys beyond the page. His copy was original. More than that, it was bloody well written."

hasn't fallen into the trap of pb's and gadgets. He embraces the idea that fishing is an adventure: a simple sport that brings people into contact with nature.

In truth, I've been a fan of his work for some time. I enjoyed his irreverent, quirky and fresh style, his ability to paint vivid pictures and take his readers on journeys beyond the page. His copy was original. More than that, it was bloody well written.

A few years on from those early pieces, Dom has a body of work that spans disciplines, species and countries, and the best of it is right here in this book.

For existing fans, you'll already know what to expect. But for those who've not read his work, you're not just in for a treat, you're about to be given a reminder that modern fishing writing doesn't have to be boring.

I'm sure you'll all enjoy the book.

Matt Hayes, October 2015

A natural high: Weed and wild carp infested Pant-y-llyn

a white van in Wales

THE STEREO IS BROKEN. THE RADIO DOESN'T TUNE. The windows don't work. Neither do the cigarette lighter or the fan, while the wing mirrors are a patchwork of gaffer tape. I could go on, but I'm starting to think it would be quicker to make a shortlist of the parts of Norbert Darby's white van that actually work than try to catalogue the defects.

It's certainly got character, I'll say that much about this rusting white vehicle. Don't ask me why, but fishing vans always seem to be white. Norbert talks to his own like it's his darling, but it is a piece of shit. "She's been running for sixteen years now," he says, and I add nothing, not wishing to tempt fate as we rattle onto the M5, two scruffy anglers in a scruffy van.

Tidy it isn't, but certainly spacious. Lying in the back in no particular order is a spectacularly random collection of two fishermen's aspirations for a weekend in Wales: rods, reels, baits, buckets and bags. In spite of this wealth of tackle, I keep glancing round and scanning the back with my usual paranoia of some small but vital item missing. Usually with Norbert there is plenty of cider and a treasury of odds and ends, but no sign of any solid food.

In between scraps of idle chatter I study the contents of the van. The sun shields conceal several dozen unopened bills and in one corner a dash of yellow with the bold letters: FIXED PENALTY NOTICE.

My head is scraping the roof because, naturally, the seats don't work. I try wrestling with the wheel thingy at the side, thrash backwards and forwards and search for non-existent levers. I'm beaten, so I ask Norbert "so how do you adjust the seats?"

He just chuckles. "You can't. I mean...they don't," he admits. So I just sit there, head wedged in place.

I was lying when I said the fan didn't work. It does. The only hitch is that it constantly blares hot air out, stuck on "slow roast" temperature. Combined with windows that are stuck solid, the effect is like sitting in a sauna with your clothes on. A little desperately I ask if the windows open. Like some kind of white van sage, Rob tells me a little mysteriously: "Yes, there is a way." The way in question involves a pair of pliers and brute force, but I manage to jam open an inch or two of space and cool air floods in.

Even more pressing than the need for air, however, is the matter of getting to Wales. I look for a map but the only printed matter I can find is a tattered copy of *Swahili for the Broken Hearted*. Not your average white van literature. With a touch of drizzle spitting down, Rob flicks the windscreen wipers on and the left blade flaps and squeaks limply like a dying bird.

An hour later we're rolling our way beyond the wide, muddy banks of the Bristol Channel, beyond the hulking concrete and steel of the great bridge and the rip-off five-quid-something toll charge. But still the wilderness must wait. If heaven is a wild lake somewhere in Wales, hell is possibly Newport Services. But needs must. Over a quick coffee I escape from the confines of Rob's white angel and try to straighten my craned neck, the blood finally returning to my feet. Along with the flaky-looking smokers and chipped picnic tables is a trio of feral cats, one no older than six months, picking through the leftovers.

Back on the road we push on into the wide open heart of Wales. Things begin to shift. The houses thin out and the trees get their revenge. There are no cash points or cul-de-sacs. No designer developments or hulking Tescos. Sadly, not many road signs either.

Mile by mile though, we edge closer to our destination, the remote lake of Pant-y-Llyn. A weedy, ancient place populated by wild carp that have been resident for centuries. It is not merely the lack of air conditioning that makes me hot and excitable. But first we must find our lake. "It could be bloody anywhere", concurs Norbert, as I make hard work of the map.

As we backtrack on ourselves after another wrong turn I pray that the rattle in the back is just a loose bit of tackle. Should the van suddenly splutter to a halt I have no idea what location we'd give the AA. I simply don't know. Norbert never knows much either. But that is essentially why we're here. Because we're sick of knowing. Bored of platformed ponds and well-worn paths. Bored of the local lakes with their weights and figures and ranks of camouflaged regulars.

THE LAKE ITSELF STARTS WITH A SLOPE. TO CALL IT A TRACK LET ALONE A ROAD WOULD BE A FILTHY LIE. The dirty white van roars and groans, shudders and rocks. Norbert, who enjoys this sort of vehicular abuse, seems oblivious while I feel every dip and bump, every rock. But by now it's too late to turn back. Suddenly we come to a halt, but it is not the terrain but the view that stops our progress.

Looming before us is an epic, boggy beast of a lake. At last, we have reached Pant-y-Llyn. A vast, prehistoric looking pool that seems more weed than water. A great bowl whose sides are broad heaths and rocky crags. "Unspoiled" doesn't come close.

And here we are in a sodding white van. It seems rude somehow, like attending a gentleman's club in a white tracksuit.

Leaving the white wonder at a healthy distance we make our descent to the shoreline below. A mere sliver of clear water circles the lake. Beyond is a tangled mass of weed thicker than a village idiot convention.

First out of the van come not rods or reels but a weed rake. It is hot, blistering work in the naked sunlight, but rake we must. The bottom clouds thick like smoke and in come clots of stringy tendrils, knots of weedy mess. Into this exercise we place our backs, our sweat and finally our bait, before the lake falls silent once more.

For almost the whole of a long, hot afternoon little happens. Swims are primed, rods are assembled. Only the breeze stirs our float tips. Every so often we are taunted by the scaly shoulder of a carp, turning in the weed beyond. Further along the bank two young children are having better luck armed with nets. Every few minutes their excited voices call out as they pick out bugs, snails and newts. And then it dawns on me that this rich soup before us provides these wild carp with all they need. Why should they eat our bait? These fish will need time to get used to bread or sweetcorn. But time, at least, is something we have plenty of. And there are worse ways to spend an evening than cracking open a cider and taking the piss out of Norbert and his van.

ONLY AS THE LIGHT DIMS A LITTLE AND THE EVENING DRAWS CLOSER DO THE CARP START TO APPEAR WITHIN REACH OF THE CLEAR FRINGES OF THE LAKE. One raked area shows billows of silt kicking up as dark shapes emerge. As we sneak into position, a fin grazes the surface.

Within seconds of lowering a bait into the water, the response is decisive. Norbert's float lifts, then plods under before the rod is almost wrestled from his hands. The calm of the lake is obliterated as our first wildie plunges headlong for several acres of dense weed.

Steady pressure avoids disaster and in spite of the inevitable collection of salad on the line, the rod still kicks with life as he wrestles the hooked fish clear. Moments later, several pounds of weed join the muscular creature in the landing net.

The wild carp is a very different creature to the fat, farmed fish we know from home. While the big mouth and whiskery barbules remain, it is a longer, sleeker creation of leathery gold scales and raw power. A strikingly long dorsal fin reaches almost right to the tail.

After we release her, the others are spooked and take a while to settle, so I must be patient for my own encounter. Bizarrely, the next battle is not with a wild carp but a 2lb chub, a mysterious presence at such a lofty place so far from the river.

The carp awaken again in the cool of the evening. Once again, the bite is decisive, a steady, almost naive sliding away followed by an explosion of heaving water. After another pulsating, tangled fight in the shallows I'm sat clutching the most primitive, whiskery-looking carp I've ever laid eyes on.

Each time a fish is hooked, the others scatter and we must move elsewhere to keep the bites coming. They fight dirty and we lose as many as we land, quickly discovering how easily a hook loses its hold when the fish find giant clots of weed.

Wild thing: a lean, long-finned carp

By about half past nine all I can see is the end of Norbert's roll-up cigarette. It's getting late but it's a struggle to tear ourselves away from the lake, back to take on the rutted track in Norbert's rusting pride and joy.

Shadows fall and in the dying light the lake resembles a huge, dark crater. As I peer back for one last glance, something rolls way out in the swampy beyond, and I'm still spellbound as the shabby white van rattles back to life. ●

it came from the drains

IT'S NOT THE MOST EXTENSIVE PIKE FISHING LOCATION YOU'VE EVER SEEN. Nor the most scenic, to be frank. Calling it a "drain" would probably be outright flattery. The odd spatter of rain adds little to the romance of the scene before us; a muddy, reedy channel perhaps five metres across. More of a ditch than a drain, you might say. Welcome to soggy Somerset.

In the trees behind I pick out the off-yellow paint of an abandoned tractor. A decrepit greenhouse and some random piping complete the picture. Had the film *Deliverance* been filmed in Somerset, this would have made a prime location. It's so rustic here the local hoodlums have resorted to throwing hay bales into the water in the absence of shopping trolleys. Nevertheless, a simple question lingers: exactly what might be lurking in this little channel?

A little inlet pipe at the head of the drain spouts a steady trickle of water. Mid-flow are signs of life at the very least, a dashing shoal of roach nosing the surface. But pike, here? It's not exactly the River Severn. You can spy leaves on the silty bottom, no more than two feet beneath the surface.

"You're taking the piss," says Ian. "We may as well fish in a garden pond." I'm about to concur when, right on cue, several little roach flip clear of the water. Am I hallucinating? Before I can pass any meaningful comment, fellow ditch hoppers Norbert Darby and Ian Nadin are launching various mutations of rubber and plastic drain-bound as an argument of the "I saw it first," variety breaks out.

The first take is as about as subtle as a Glasgow kiss, a wild smash on the rod tip as Ian latches into a feisty ditch pike. Seconds later the line goes slack, the look of surprise-cum-total disbelief still fixed on his face. The very idea of pike in this Lilliput-sized water is no longer a cider-fuelled fantasy but fact.

We're still shaking our heads as we trundle off down the drain casting as we go. But perhaps the existence of fish, including the apex predator itself, should not come as such a shock in these small, sometimes tiny, channels. Aside from the bigger and better known Somerset drains, the region is packed with countless smaller rhynes, ditches and culverts. As they criss-cross, merge and interlink, the fish inevitably also spill over into all kinds of unexpected places, the annual floods further mixing up this strange labyrinth of water and reeds, mud and fish.

Even after witnessing a pike attack you still can't help feeling daft at times. In

Dinner for one:
Norbert ponders today's debris

parts there is barely a foot of water and you could reach the far bank with a short leap, never mind a short cast. It goes without saying that in most cases the pike are no monsters. A real leviathan would struggle to turn round in some of these locations, although there are often plenty of rudd, frogs and other goodies to feed on. "No monsters," is quite an understatement all the same; some of the pike we witness are hardly bigger than our lures.

It is where these waters widen and join broader stretches that you can and do find more substantial pike. In our case, we get excited when we reach another drain, this time one you can't jump across. Still plenty of cover, but a little more depth greets us. As with all fishing on the Levels though, there is no substitute for mobility. Your attitude should be simple: explore everything. It's a task well suited to two or three leap-frogging companions. The banter also keeps you on your toes during the slower parts of the day.

Right where we meet with the bigger drain is a pikey-looking spot in itself—an obvious ambush point for predators that can intercept fish traffic coming from either body of water. Like on a busy road, the junction is the place where there's always the threat of a messy accident. Norbert quickly confirms this with a hungry jack that's all teeth and no manners, a thin and mean-looking attacker that doesn't hesitate for a second but simply launches itself headlong at the lure from right under his feet.

FURTHER ALONG THE BANK THE TERRAIN GETS INCREASINGLY CONFUSING ONCE AGAIN. Huge heaps of dug peat break up the flat landscape, whilst behind us is an excavated site that has developed into a flooded, overgrown haven of reeds and water. I would be tempted to call it a lake, only there's no telling where it begins and ends, the very notion of such boundaries an alien concept in this sprawling landscape. Each of us is thinking the same thing, but the only fisher able to access this tangled little haven is the heron we can see, motionless at the far edge. I watch him jealously for a

In backwater Somerset, life's a ditch

few minutes, absent-mindedly wondering whether to return some other day with a chainsaw.

The drain begins to tow in the midday sun. The peat-stained water turns muddier and with bites scarce we swap and switch our lures. My own preference is for something bright and bold. Sometimes, I reason, the pike need not so much an easy meal as a great big neon sign that reads "eat here!". A rattling, orange jerkbait cuts a fine dash through the murk, gliding and swooping left to right. I flip out a short cast to some rushes. Nothing happens. With the next 20 casts nothing happens either. In fact, it is only half an hour later as I'm wondering what could possibly mistake this spotted orange oddity for a meal that I get the shock

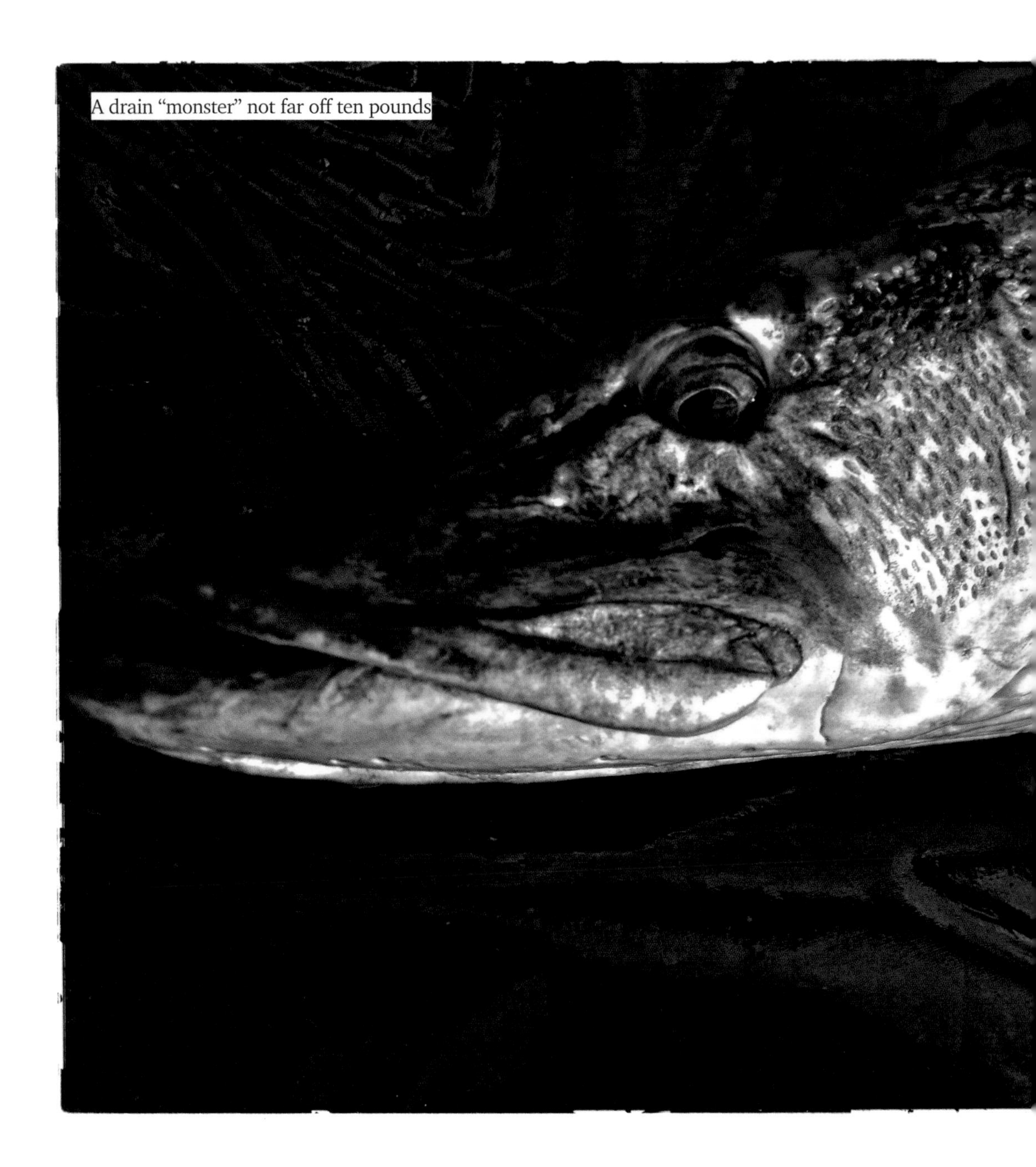
A drain "monster" not far off ten pounds

of my life. From beneath a gallery of dying reed stems, out slides a solid, mottled flank. Jaws flair and the jerkbait disappears in an almighty slash. The pike feels the tension and plunges toward the deep middle of the drain, the reel clutch buzzing in discomfort. The fight is a gripping if short-lived affair. As Ian reaches me with the net she gives a titanic shake of the head, attempting to wallow under the bank. I hold firm and she comes up to the surface, a classic drain pike: long and lean, emerald and peat-stained gold. The jerkbait is still hidden from view, lost somewhere in the toothy hollow of a cavernous, oversized head. Thankfully the hooks are debarbed and after a brief

encounter with some forceps I'm holding the fish back in the water. She can't be much bigger than 8 or 9lb, but for such a small drain this is an epic monster.

A few other arguments ensue with these backwater pike, enough at least to keep a trio of restless anglers excited on a cool afternoon. More detours are taken. More reeds and muddy miles; more bad directions and places not on the map. The day is full of surprises, some less savoury than others. In a network of water that could have been devised by a mad scientist, water levels rise and fall unpredictably from day to day, depositing all kinds of strange debris on this exposed landscape. Today's treasures include a VHS video cassette, assorted car parts and a single hotdog sausage in a jar.

"Which drain is this?" asks Norbert at one point. I shrug my shoulders. With the light starting to go it is high time to return to the world we came from, where things are better mapped but less exciting, cleaner and more predictable. If we stay much longer, we may never find our way back. "We really should get going," warns Ian. I nod my head, before making yet another "last" cast. ●

IF THE WORLD OF FISHING IS ONE OF THOSE FEW DOMAINS WHERE YOU STILL FIND THE ODD GENUINE ECCENTRIC, Scottish angler and fly tyer Leon Guthrie is probably better placed in the "certified mad" category. From a small house somewhere in Scotland, he inhabits another world of mothballs, strange materials and even stranger ideas. As I type this I can picture his desk of random threads, wings, legs and half-finished flies; a half-finished cup of tea and clippings on a dusty floor. And then there are the messages he sends me, GENERALLY ALL IN CAPITAL LETTERS, AS IF HE WERE SHOUTING FROM A VERY LONG DISTANCE AWAY.

Leon refers to himself as an alien, as you might too had you been born with six fingers on each hand. At times during correspondence, you wonder who

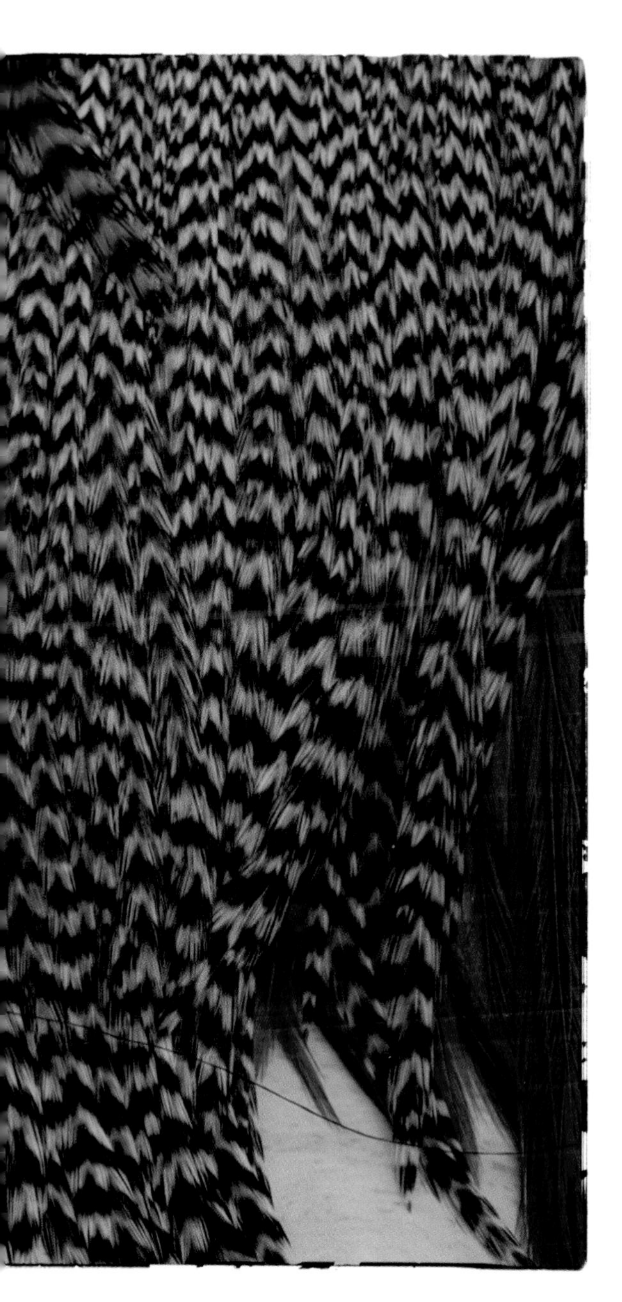

you might be talking to. A sculptor? A deerstalker from the wild country? He has lived in many guises, while his career as a commercial diver took him hundreds of feet under the sea fixing oilrigs; a risky business that played havoc with his body. To this day I cannot say whether the pressure might have affected his mind, or whether you have to be mad in the first place to lead such a life.

The flies themselves are random, manic treasures. They delight and baffle you in equal measure. There are flying insects, trapped in time; rows of salmon and trout flies sitting like birds. But look closer and you might also find an Earthworm, a Haggis or a Fried Egg.

There is a leftfield humour at play, but Leon is deadly serious about his craft. What is his motivation, I wonder? A galaxy of new flies stem chiefly from a childlike love of experimentation. He also plays with traditional flies, but there is a healthy lack of that cautious instinct within most of us, that says: "No, that's not in the rules."

"The anticipation of waiting for a fish to take one of my creations is still a delight," he says, although he adds that "basic simplicity in design catches more fish than complex, good-looking patterns."

In spite of the slick-looking flies, Leon was a relative latecomer to fly tying, I'm curious to learn. Recent poor health hasn't dampened his humour or enthusiasm and his collection of brilliant, sometimes bizarre patterns continues to grow by the day.

Any fly fisher unfamiliar with Leon's work could do worse than start with his vast range of buzzers, which range from the beautiful to the very basic. His most telling nymph pattern of all falls into the former category: the Enamel Wire Bloodworm is a mere size 10 hook and turns of wire coated in red enamel paint. Otherwise there are both deadly and deadpan statements. Coral snake colours sit next to skinny black and red nymphs, while others have the team colours of Celtic and Rangers. He also shows me a Credit Crunch Special for the recession; if you hadn't already guessed, it's just a bare hook.

Simplicity is also the key to his other nymphs, which owe as much a debt to

Creations from the simple to the unhinged:
Deadly buzzers…

…a nymph made
entirely of grass…

…Leon's Canary
(from a series of birds)

nature as to his imagination. "You don't always have to look for something pretty in your box that catches the eye," he believes. Nature is not always flamboyant, after all. On the contrary, subtlety is more often the order of the day and like any keen stream life imitator, Leon is keen to take his cue from first-hand observation. With his health somewhat fragile in recent times, the task of finding sample specimens for inspiration has sometimes fallen to his grandchildren, who have been dutifully bringing him suitable "beasties" from the stream in jam jars.

"Fish are naturally curious. Provided it looks edible, they'll take almost anything," states Leon. It's a point he illustrates with a little anecdote: "Once on the Tweed River an angler questioned me about this statement. So I asked him to gather me some dead grass stems. I had a vice in my car and tied some of the grass on a wee size 12 hook. Nothing fancy, just a little body and a tail. I told him to cast that into the Tweed. Within a handful of tries he hooked a nice trout, much to his surprise!"

Looking further into Leon's collection however, it is the outlandish flies that cause the viewer to stop and stare. Many have the eye of an artist or model maker, besides a fly tyer. His Golden Fleece is a bushy, bright nymph; the Vampire is a sinuous black lure with the white of a tooth and a spatter of blood.

DEEPER INTO THE RECESSES OF LEON GUTHRIE'S FLY BOXES, THINGS GET EVEN STRANGER. A full gallery of oddities includes a Breaded Haddock, Dyson Vacuum Cleaner, Big Mac, Bird's Nest, Cessna Aeroplane and the planet Mars. Aside from the zany humour, Guthrie's skill with epoxy in forming these fiendish things is truly something to be marvelled at.

"It's always nice when someone asks what you caught a fish on and the answer is a Big Mac or miniature aircraft."

The Dyson even has a little plug. I'm also taken by Leon's cute series of flies based on popular British birds, which includes an eagle, magpie, robin and even a seagull. I'm relieved to hear that no golden eagle feathers were used.

I'm dying to ask the next question: has Leon lost the plot with these surreal pieces, or is this art? Do these patterns actually work? The answer is surprisingly an affirmative: "Most of my novelty patterns like the Big Mac, Cessna, Bird's Nest and the others have caught fish in the past," he explains, although he makes a clear distinction between stocked and wild trout.

"We all possess curiosity," Leon puts it. "Animals, including fish, also share this quality. So you construct patterns that will induce this curiosity into a reaction to investigate. I have produced some rather odd-looking creations," he smiles. "But a laugh a day keeps the reaper at bay, as I always put it. It's always nice when someone asks what you caught a fish on and the answer is a Big Mac or miniature aircraft. By the time they stop laughing, they're probably wondering if I'm right in the head."

Traditionalists may scoff, but Leon's work reminds us of something important: making flies is meant to be fun. It's meant to be creative and individual. It needn't be a cold church with dogmatic rules. And where a lot of us stick to the prescribed formula, Leon is constantly prepared to take risks and approach things from a fresh angle. Adapt and improve, reinvent and create from scratch, he continues to throw the rulebook into the loch and go boldly where others fear to tread.

You might easily call Leon Guthrie an eccentric. But then again, you might also come to a simple but startling realisation: that anything is possible from the basic starting point of a hook in a vice. "It is quite amazing how many new designs can be created on a simple piece of wire," says Leon. And in spite of the thousands of bewildering flies in his collection, I get the feeling he is only just getting started. ●

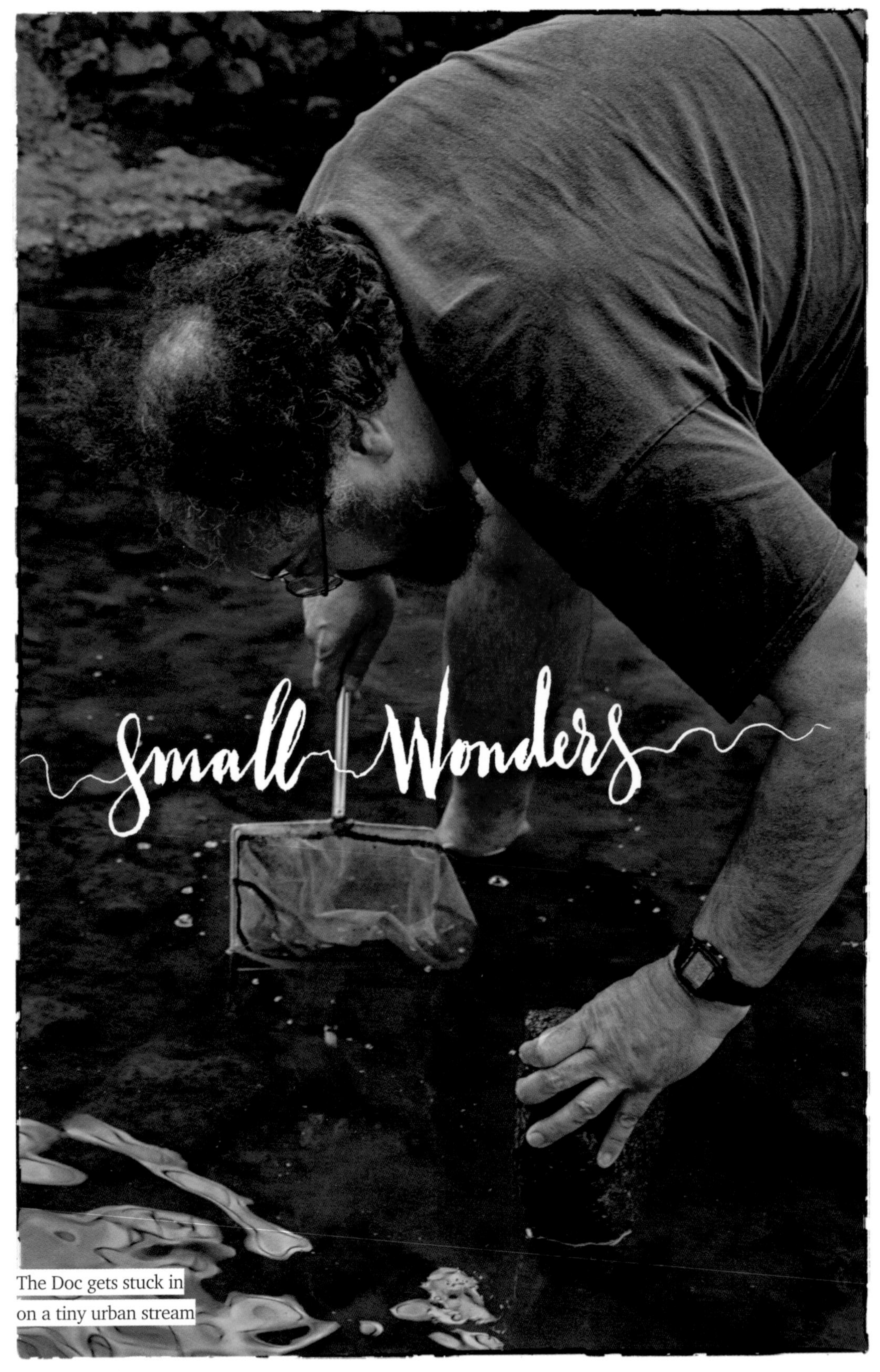

The Doc gets stuck in on a tiny urban stream

THE CALL OF "CATCH BIGGER" IS JUST ABOUT EVERYWHERE YOU LOOK IN THE FISHING WORLD THESE DAYS. We travel miles and spend small fortunes in pursuit of the big one. But be honest, did you ever secretly crave a return to simpler fishing? Did you ever miss those smaller fish and more innocent times?

We might spend whole weekends waiting for the fish that fills the net and makes our mates jealous, but for most of us it all started with the smaller stuff. A daft gudgeon, sticklebacks in a jam jar or the hordes of suicidally bold minnows my brothers would count, racking up cricket scores.

If you look a little closer, these little gems are still there to be found beneath random bridges, in village ponds, the ragged stream by the curry house or any of the other magical and haphazard spots where Dr Mark Everard is to lead us in a search for small things. It might not be macho to fish for creatures that would often fit in a matchbox, but there are entire little worlds to be discovered. Using our hands and feet, nets, strings, poles and traps we will try to find answers and perhaps even scoop a little lost youth into the bottom of a bucket.

The plan for our own mini species hunt began three summers or so ago, as I struck up a conversation with Mark having enjoyed his fascinating *Little Book of Little Fishes*. With both of us rather jaded at the lack of soul in so much of the current fishing scene, we decided that it would be fun to launch a specimen hunt on a different scale.

DR EVERARD'S HOUSE SITS IN A SLEEPY VILLAGE BY THE BRISTOL AVON, and is a kind of happy-go-lucky mixture of science and anarchy. There are books, guitars and journals in droves; a poster of the Tree of Life, plant diagrams and no fewer than five fish tanks. Daisy, his teenage daughter, is lounging in the garden along with a black and white cat, as we round up minnow traps, quiver tips and tiny hooks.

Also joining us will be the General, who at just six inches tall could make even the smallest fish look like a world-beater. I enlisted him when it struck me that even the biggest ruffe or minnow wouldn't look very impressive in my own cumbersome hands. I found the General at a car boot sale for the grand sum of 20p and straight away, I knew I had my man. With a camo-green uniform, outstretched arms and the fixed, joyless grimace of a true big fish angler he was the perfect candidate. But for good measure, Mark also picks out a 1960s model Dalek for an even dafter fishing prop, both of us probably showing our level of maturity.

With equipment thrown in the car, our tour begins with a tiny pond beside the village cricket pitch. It is hopelessly overgrown, and the nettles sting the shit out of my legs as we look for a way in. We have a net and a bucket and are probably too excited for grown men.

"This is where it all started for me," he says. "With sticklebacks, a branch and a worm. They grabbed hold so aggressively you didn't even need a hook," he reflects, as he sweeps a net in the black water.

A diminutive pond might promise little, but in effect each is its own ecosystem. Life finds a way, if you are a tiny opportunist like a three-spined stickleback. But in our case, the summer water level has dropped so low the task proves fruitless. I guess every specimen hunter draws a blank sometimes.

Undimmed, we make our way to the outskirts of town, where an urban stream trickles between narrow streets and parked

Tiddler bashing on the Bristol Avon

cars. This time there is more promise, as life flickers amidst the stones. Mark plays a game of cat and mouse with a bucket in one hand and a net in the other, resembling a giant in this tiny stream, as the tiddlers flee like sparks around his feet.

Whether you are six or 56, catching bullheads requires quick hands and a little strategy. A strange, speckled kind of freshwater blenny, these creatures hide on the bottom and are quick to take cover. But by lifting a stone and having a net smartly placed to intercept the fleeing bullhead, you have a chance.

In spite of its tiny size and secretive nature, the fish also known as the sculpin, or "miller's thumb", is a voracious predator with a big head and a bad attitude. By his carefully cupped hands, I know Mark has scored this time. Even in the hands of the General they are small fish, but my macro

Mark admires a shimmering bleak

The bullhead is a nostalgic favourite

lens captures paddle fins, froggy eyes and a neatly freckled camouflage.

We also look to add a stone loach to the bucket, but these are as skinny as they are evasive and, slightly ominously, the most conspicuous residents of all here are the signal crayfish. You can find these horrible, clawed invaders in just about any hole or crevice and those we find are dutifully stomped on, not without a slightly brutal sense of relish.

LARGER SIGNS OF LIFE AWAIT FURTHER DOWN THE ROAD AS WE TAKE A DETOUR TO THE WINDING BRISTOL AVON. Mark might be a doctor, but still has that true angler's affliction of wanting to study and stare into every little culvert, cut, ditch and brook they come across. Beside a pillared bridge we ditch the nets in favour of light stick floats and maggots. The bites come rapidly, mostly from dace and greedy young chub.

The bane of minnows, Dr Mark Everard

The float just keeps dipping, but we have an unusual problem for anglers: the fish are too big, we want smaller.

A bleak is our next mini-species, and not a bad one either. No great angling feat, but these are vivid little fish with a shimmer of silver, blue and green-gold. In the arms of the General, it looks like a bloody tarpon.

Other fish are also present on the river, but the most effective strategy doesn't involve a rod, but a bottle trap positioned in the shallows. Mark has the sort of minnow catching device you last saw in a kid's book, complete with string and bait. Left in the current for just 10 minutes, the speckled little thieves come rushing in to take the bread.

Cupping a hand over the hole, Mark brings up a haul of some two-dozen minnows. Some of them shoot around in alarm, while the rest just keep eating the bread. There must be literally millions of these fish in the river system, and while they might be common, they are undeniably pretty.

Our friend the Doctor actually once caught a British record minnow, although he laughs at himself at the mention of it. "I was actually playing in a band, the night before," he says, "and it was one of those nights we were all up late after the gig. It must have been about three in the morning when I joked that I was going to catch a record minnow."

The titanic specimen came from a cut off pond, where just a handful of minnows had escaped during a flood. With the water rich with daphnia (water fleas) and other food, the minnows had grown greedy and fat. At 15g, it was witnessed by the drummer, and joked about for weeks afterwards.

A mighty gudgeon for the General

ON A BAKING AFTERNOON, WE MUST TRAVEL FURTHER TO FIND OTHER SMALL DELIGHTS. But as we cast our attention wider the venue is, if anything, even narrower as we make our way to where the Somerset Coal Canal meets the Kennet and Avon. It's a baking hot walk as we approach the soaring heights of the Dundas Aqueduct. The weather is fine and the canal looks pretty—a fact not lost on the boating parties, ice cream sellers and assorted walkers on the towpath. And into the mix, we throw pole rigs, split shot, maggots and a centrepin reel.

Our afternoon fish off will be a celebration of simplicity and variety, as testified by Mark's lengthy answer when an old chap asks: "What do you actually catch here?" The correct answer could be anything, with a couple of float fished maggots in the right place, but our spot just by the mouth of a turning bay is teeming with bleak and dace as we arrive.

Canal dace? There are so many here that the float barely settles. Nor are their bright silver and blue colours marred by the busy, murky waters here. Roach join them too, with the inevitable miniscule but devilishly greedy perch and some beautiful little gudgeon. Some of the fish look a bit on the small side even when cradled by the General or a pint-sized toy Dalek frankly, but it's such addictively simple fun we're not bothered.

However, what I am really hoping for is a ruffe. Not so common these days and altogether absent in my home county of Devon, these cute, perch-like fish are something of a mystery to me. But for the time being, my childish daydreams are rudely interrupted by the boat traffic churning its way through. I add a little

A fine way to waste an afternoon

more groundbait after every one that passes, as stag night parties drink tinned lager and accidentally smash the paint off the sides of hired narrowboats.

The little fish just keep coming regardless, for most of the day. Most of them would fit on a beer mat, with the possible exception of a flawless 2lb hybrid that makes Mark's centrepin reel spin and the net bulge, before being derided as a "nuisance fish".

Meanwhile, I reclaim my love of pole fishing for small fish, something I should enjoy more often. But where are these ruffe? I suggest to Mark that they have all been grilled and eaten by Romanians, presumably on very small barbeques. But eventually, another bold as you like bite for Mark results in a hoot of excitement along the bank and the magic word "ruffe!"

From the size of the thing alone we're probably a bit overexcited. But the ruffe is more than just a runty little half-perch half-gudgeon type creature. It is a forgotten extra as far as our native species go. But what a beautiful little fish the ruffe is in the palm of the hand: a spiny, speckled creature that, in spite of its measly size, is an avid predator.

Aside from the odd dodgy accidental water where pike anglers have emptied a bait can, the ruffe has dwindled in many rivers and canals, suffering from environmental decline or gobbled up by the spread of zander. It is unusual to find them anywhere in the West Country, but on this particular canal a few ruffe managed to sneak their way into the canal among a stocking of silver fish, before quickly multiplying.

The speckled Ruffe is an irresistibly cute throwback to more innocent times

Further ruffe move in and it is soon my turn to receive a bold bite. They thump quite beautifully on light tackle and can look quite impressive, at least in the hands of a six-inch tall plastic army general. They also posses a certain, not unattractive, alien quality to my unfamiliar eye. The exaggerated mouth and eyes remind you of perch. So does the spiky fin on the back—although in the case of ruffe, the two dorsal fins are oddly fused together. The colours are rich too, if you look closer: hues of green and gold mix with silver and yellow, while the cute flecks of camouflage look as if they had been applied with a pepper shaker.

The early evening is sultry as the canal gets quieter and we must think about leaving. "One more fish"becomes our mantra and as we struggle to pull ourselves away, I can't help but wonder what happened to the fishing world of my childhood, when anglers would happily spend an afternoon catching roach, dace, gudgeon or whatever came along?

Our full day of tiddler bashing seems to have passed in a flash, perhaps like all truly enjoyable time spent on the bank. And although our catches might not be big or especially clever, we have used more methods, caught more species and enjoyed more twists, turns and detours than just about any fishing trip in my life.

Perhaps it takes something of a child's eye, but beyond the bragging rights and the army of big fish obsessives, there are still cute corners to be discovered and an innocence that can be rekindled with the simple dip of a float. ●

the curse of the towpath

OF ALL THE PLACES THAT TURN ANGLERS INTO FANATICS, A SHIP CANAL HAS TO BE PRETTY LOW ON THE LIST. We're not here for the scenery, the rusting lock gates or the overpriced beer at the Double Locks Inn. Exeter Ship Canal cuts a wide and weedy five miles or so from city to salt water. It is a fearsomely deep, and sometimes fearsomely difficult challenge.

But I've seen them. Carp so solid they leave you mesmerised. Down by the waterworks you can spot hulking, barrel-thick fish nosing through the clear water. On sunny days you pick out dark backs and dense shoulders; gaping mouths that could swallow your fist. These are kind of carp that have consumed whole summers, flattened bank balances and ended relationships. And I want to catch one. Badly.

But out on this semi urban canal, it isn't just carp that make you hold your breath. I

"As any diehard
angler understands,
for the possibility
of sudden elation to
exist there must also
be the possibility of
failure."

don't know many anglers who would park their car overnight here, never mind camp out and fish. A friend and a blunt object are necessities, here in the vicinity of the city's fag end as we join a cast of boy racers, drunks and the odd lost lunatic. Or is that us?

Rob Darby, better known as "Norbert", is my usual towpath companion, and an angler of unfailing humour but dubious reliability. Over a cold drink, tackle is prepared, tactics are discussed and we dare once again to dream of vast, unfathomable carp. Theories are outlined, debated and abandoned; cigarettes are rolled, stories swapped and mosquitoes swatted.

Our little camp is already well established from several post-work sessions, as we sit unshaven like the disciples of some muddy cult. We dodge dog shit as Norbert cracks open another cider. The grass we sit on, like my patience, is thinning. Not that we're short on time. On the contrary, there's plenty of it. Time to hope and time to doubt. Time to speculate, perhaps to laugh at the whole exercise. Time itself can become heavy. The more nights you spend the more hell bent you become on seeing the plan through. But for what, exactly?

Certain lessons are learned the hard way, admittedly. Tiger nuts become the bait of choice above boilies, after my bream in the silly hours of the morning become a running joke. Prebaiting is a must too, if you hope to wean these carp off their natural diet. And while any fool can subdue a big fish in a featureless pond, the stupendously thick weed here makes anything but the toughest tackle a liability. So yes, we're great on the theory, just not so hot on catching anything.

The sun glows red before it drowns on the water. The moon is up and in the fading light you can follow the bridge in the distance, hear the hiss of the road, now and again the wayward howl of a siren. And here we are like hitchhikers stuck on a verge, a thin strip of green between canal and river, steel barrier one side, a long and muddy drop on the other. But these are things I try not to dwell on.

THE ELECTRICITY PYLONS LOOM IN A GREAT ROW THROUGH THE FIELDS ACROSS THE RIVER BEHIND US. A jury of cormorants span the wires like bad language scrawled on black lines. It's the wait that is the real test, the real killer. Hanging about and hoping. Waking up in the drizzle and waiting, always waiting. But perhaps it's the chasm between a huge fish and absolutely nothing that compels us. As any diehard angler understands, for the possibility of sudden elation to exist there must also be the possibility of failure.

The statistics alone are lethal. Taking a sip from a dirty mug, Norbert attempts the

Reward at last: a hard-won mirror carp

mathematics of the impossible: six nights; two rods per man; around 10 kilos of bait; 30 or so mozzie bites; several litres of tea and 100 of Norbert's skinny roll-ups. Three dozen or so casts for that paltry vital figure: one lost carp. Hooked for all of 30 glorious seconds before becoming nothing more than slack line and words I can't repeat. We have prime baits and specimen tackle, lonely partners and empty wallets. But we still don't have our carp.

By 11, the cold really draws in. By slow turns everything grows quieter. Even the boy racers get bored until it's just me, Norbert and the mozzies left. Insect repellent is as important as any rod or reel here once darkness descends.

"It'll happen at some point. It's only a matter of time," I say. It's not the first, or even the second or third time I've used that line, along with the classic: "All it takes is one bite." But after another blank night, the talk is on the Curse of the Towpath. And sometimes as I lie there sleeplessly, I wonder if it's true and that we'll spend half of eternity here. It's even harder to drop off

peacefully after Norbert recalls the night he saw a drunken transvestite wandering along the towpath.

"Feeling lucky tonight, sir?" he asks me.

"Piss off, Norbert."

IT'S ONLY AFTER A SPECULATIVE NIGHT ON ANOTHER PATCH, MILES AWAY FROM THE LAST USELESS SWIM, THAT SOMETHING DECISIVE FINALLY OCCURS. Following a row with his other half, Norbert snores as he lies in a heap on my groundsheet and I'm in that zone where I try to sleep, but have a funny feeling something is about to happen. But for now it doesn't.

Morning emerges by slow degrees. It's not yet light, but soon it'll be time to pack up and be away. So I'm just lying there, wondering about things. Whether to go for a leak, or whether the carp are somewhere else entirely. And that's when it happens. With no warning whatsoever the alarm goes berserk and I see the line racing tight. I'm stumbling forward with no shoes, no second thoughts, on hands and knees grabbing the rod and holding on. The bend is deep and urgent as the fish plunges sideways, already several yards down the canal. The drag sputters for a few seconds before the only sensation is a dense, motionless weight.

The weed on the canal is chronic in summer, and by this stage I'm fearing the worst. I keep a tight line and pray the fish is still there. For perhaps five minutes all I get is the occasional thump to reassure me we're still connected. It's only as I walk down the bank and change the angle that the fish finally bolts for the central channel again and I breathe a huge sigh of relief. As positively as I dare, the fish is guided slowly towards the bank. Along with about half its own weight in weed, she slides into the net and the universe seems to freeze.

I shout out loud; Norbert looks almost confused. The fish in the net is a fantastically solid mirror carp, all gaping mouth and gold scales. It looks as surprised as us. At 15lb-something I'm not about to win any awards, but can perhaps be forgiven for feeling slightly delirious. All the nights on the bank; years of watching these solid, somehow untouchable fish in the canal and longing to catch one.

What seemed impossible only hours ago now lies in my hands and the only thing that could make my life complete is a fried breakfast. I'm already looking forward to the call from my brother and the usual question: "You're not still fishing that bloody canal for carp are you?" ●

WITH FEW EXCEPTIONS, MOST OF US ARE FORCED TO FIT OUR FISHING AROUND THE DAILY GRIND. If I could spend half the hours fishing that I did working, I would be a happier, saner man. Most afternoons, however, my fishing takes place only in daydreams.

Quiet lakes and dipping floats are imagined during coffee breaks, pauses in phone calls, traffic jams. There is always the thought that, far from the tepid coffee, junk emails and looming deadlines, the water is exactly as you left it, serene and inviting. While I am filling in reports, tench are bubbling in the margins. As I'm talking to the boss, the bass are prowling the rocks and trout are rising on the stream.

But these are idle dreams that can't escape a universal truth; someone has to crack the

whip, someone has to shovel the shit. You wonder just how all those who fish right through the week manage it, but I regard them with a measure of envy and distrust.

Only on one or two occasions have I given my skiving tendencies free reign and actually fled the office for the river bank. Rather than feeling nagging guilt, I have come to a different conclusion; sometimes the best hours by the water are those that are stolen.

It is September. My job has been about as rewarding as backache, all summer long. It would be so easy to snatch a day off. Easy and guilt free. At least, that's what I keep telling myself. The thought has been tormenting me for a while. Just keep your bottle, dial the number and talk in a croaky voice that suggests impending tragedy. It's an easy decision really: another day making up the numbers in a tie, or up to your knees in cool, trickling water, taking in the last day of the trout season. The die is cast.

As soon as the rush hour ebbs away, I jump out of bed, cured of my terminal illness. I kick today's post under the stairs, switch my mobile off and throw it into the laundry basket. Seizing my stream rod and a box of flies, I throw together a small but decadent lunch. Before you can say "workshy", I'm hurtling out of the city towards greener pastures, flying like a bird from a cage, far from Mr Perry and his soul-deflating business jargon, far from the crushing small talk of the office, far beyond all reach of faxes, phones and memos.

With everyone at work, the country roads are deserted. I cackle wickedly at the simple audacity of my plan and the fact that no one will ever suspect a thing, grin smugly at business news on the Beeb, the working nation, the crappy empire of nine to five, a place that seems so, so far from the more peaceful rush of an autumn river. Is this what freedom feels like?

The sun is breaking through the office grey sky as I tackle up by a little stone bridge. Even having made my getaway, I want to remain invisible, existing only as an angler, so I scribble the name "I.Walton"

on my ticket and drop it into the cobwebs of the tin collection box.

My fingers tremble with more than the effects of coffee and cigarettes as I tackle up. When the river looks so perfect I'm always in a terrible hurry. I pass a hasty line through the rings and select a fine leader.

By the stream, everything changes. I breathe a little deeper and pause for enlightenment as I study the contents of my fly box. This morning, the dull routine of the workplace has been replaced by the grace of the river.

As a fly fisherman I now work to a far slower clock. No one dictates the tempo of my day and I intend to keep it as laid back and unruffled as the river itself. I begin by the bridge, wading gently into the water. The level is still low, but the day is warm and the water is clear. I steadily get into my rhythm, throwing measured, short casts, enjoying the flex of the little rod. Thirty miles away my chair is empty, my coffee cup dry. The hours will pass steadily and uneventfully as usual back at work; but today I am not going to spend the day checking the clock. I take off my watch and tuck the fly rod under my arm to roll a cigarette and watch the water.

THE RIVER LACKS ITS RUDE SUMMER HEALTH TODAY, BEAUTIFUL THOUGH IT IS. Green is giving way to brown, the air noticeably cooler. Insects are scarce on the water and rising fish scarcer still. I tell myself that the trout are still here somewhere. Only a few weeks ago they were clearly visible everywhere you looked. Perhaps this is some kind of payback for my indolence? More likely, these little browns are not prepared to venture far from the stony riverbed to snatch a dry fly, so logic points towards a wet. A gold ribbed spider catches my eye, at least. The fibres breathe and

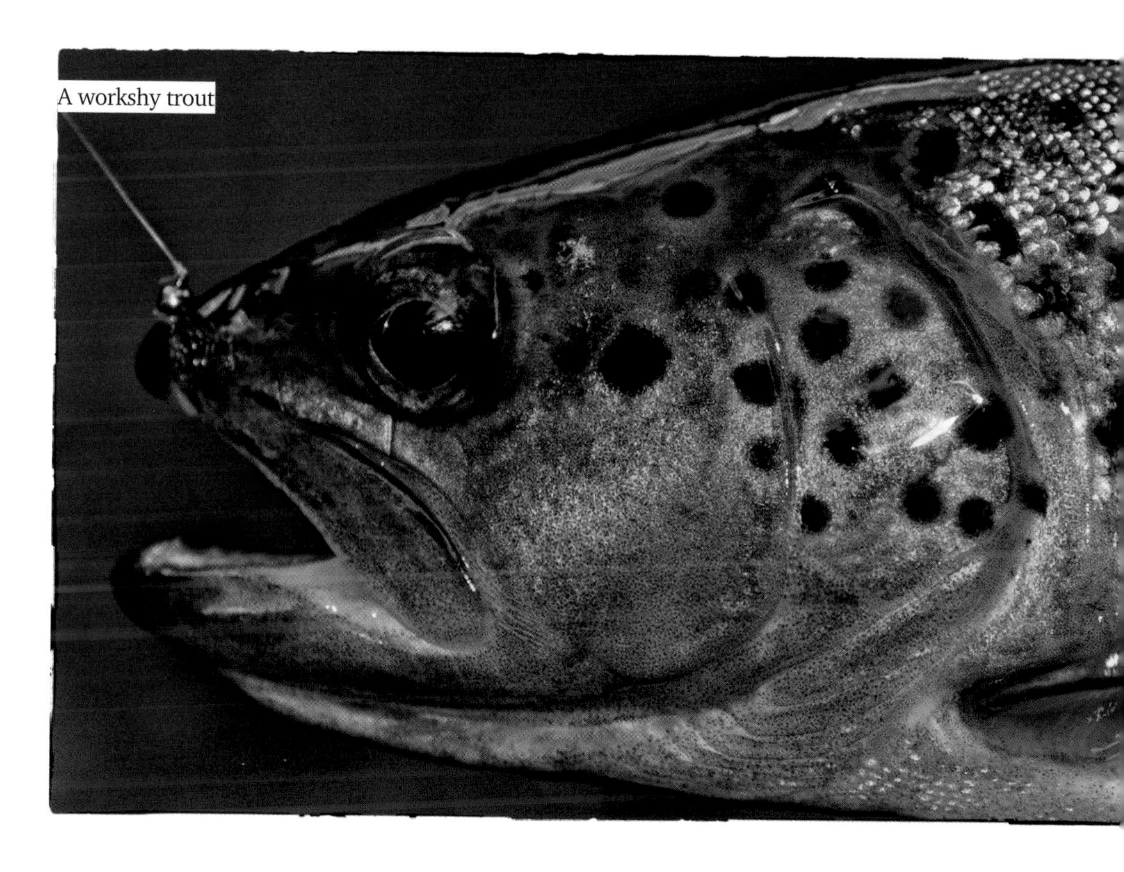
A workshy trout

dance in the current. I let it sink freely for a few seconds on its way through a tree-lined run and, finally, the line tingles and the little rod judders into life.

There is a coppery flash in the tea-coloured water. The fish is beautiful but too small to merit the net. He fits perfectly in the hand, with colours as rich as autumn leaves. I keep hold for a few seconds in the current before he is gone, merging with the stony bottom once again.

For the rest of the afternoon I roam slowly upstream, casting and just watching the water. I keep searching and pondering, only sparing a passing thought for the workers bound for home and the dour symphony of the rush hour building once again. The trout are in a temperamental mood today, but this is one line of work I enjoy. More glides, pools and eddies are explored, each bringing the promise of fresh discovery. Most of the time my nymphs sail by unmolested, but I remain happy with just the moment and the possibility of another take. And for a time, work doesn't exist. Nor do stress, the government, the neighbours, traffic, anything. It's just this river. That's it.

I wait until evening before I think about leaving. Driving past workmates with a car full of fishing stuff wouldn't look very clever. Two more trout grab the fly late afternoon, leaping and turning in the stream. As the day begins to darken I find it hard to pull myself away from the river. I count the minutes and curse a missed rise. I get a vague, empty longing in my belly. I know that soon I will have to bid the river goodbye until next year. I will have return to the city and address my chronic lack of ambition once again. I will have to make a magical recovery from pretend sickness. I will have to head back to the world of council tax, cars and careers. This is called freedom. ●

Mullet therapy

THEY'RE ELEGANT, LITHE AND POWERFUL. They have sleek lines and weird heads. Tourists enjoy ogling them every summer as they swim around harbours and seafronts in naked view from Brighton Marina to Barcelona, driving small boys to distraction and grown men to drink. With a fickle nature and a name that makes you think of Chris Waddle circa 1986, mullet are the scourge of countless anglers every summer, myself included.

A dirty game: spinning on a tidal river

"Do these fish actually eat anything? Or do they just lark about in the mud, feeding on human despair?"

Sometimes, quite frankly, you wonder why you bother in the first place. Perhaps no other fish more clearly illustrates the gulf between seeing your quarry and catching it. That first sight of a mullet shoal is glorious. You spot them everywhere, twatting about without a care in the world. "This is going to be easy!" you think. Four hours and several abandoned plans later as you're still sat there watching them, a question hangs in your mind: do these fish actually eat anything? Or do they just lark about in the mud, feeding on human despair?

"The British Bonefish" is a particularly crap nickname for the species. Utter nonsense. Sure, they fight hard. But bonefish actually eat things other than mud and microscopic organisms. If mullet truly were like bonefish, our seaside towns would be crammed with Orvis-endorsed guides and glass-bottomed skiffs. Well-heeled Americans would strut around Torquay and Christchurch in designer shades saying "Gee, there goes a British Bonefish." The more modest "Grey Ghost" nickname I can handle, because ghosts also crop up in crumbling seaside towns and eat sod all.

No, these are not bonefish, but bizarre, infuriating creatures that are a little like the British summer itself; a promise that rarely quite materialises. One summer in particular sticks in my mind with confounding clarity. I

The baited spinner, a canny trick for the frustrated mullet fisher

had been camping in France with a mate and we were hypnotised by dozens of them in a little harbour. We tried bread and maggots, floats and swimfeeders. We tore our hair out on a daily basis as we watched them piss around playfully and defy logic itself. Just what do these buggers even eat? Even worse, my first success was accidental, casting from a sea wall with a huge worm on a size 2/0 hook. The take itself nearly pulled the rod in. What I thought would be a 5lb bass turned into an average-sized mullet—and what should have represented a big victory only seemed further confirmation that mullet were invented by the devil to torment fishermen.

One afternoon as we watched the local netsmen, they didn't seem much more successful. We saw men wading with a traditional seine net and trap a group of fish. But every time they closed the trap, just about every member of the shoal would jump clear of the water and make good their escape.

MY OWN FRUSTRATION WITH MULLET LED ME TO SEEK ALTERNATIVE MEANS. Netting, explosives and fish-hypnotism are all banned in Devon however, so instead I took notes from local members of the National Mullet Club. It might sound like a society for people with terrible haircuts, but its members are a breed apart when it comes to these odd fish. And appropriately enough, the best mullet angler I found, Mr Bert Brockington, is also a trained counselor, who grins wryly as he tells me "a lot of the time with mullet, it's me who needs the therapy".

As many readers will know, mullet are one of two main types: thin or thick-lipped.

Revenge is sweet

Both will take bait (allegedly) but for reasons which still escape me, thin-lipped mullet will also take a baited spinner. And it was this cunning trick, recommended by Bert, that probably delivered me from madness.

The method itself is simple enough. First, you take a small to mid-sized spinner and crop off the treble hook. In its place goes a single hook attached to two or three inches of fluorocarbon, braid or fine wire. If you can find a long-shanked baitholder hook pattern in a smallish size, so much the better. Onto the hook is threaded your worm bait. A whole small redworm, or part of a lob or rag is perfect, although ragworms are better when you're nearer to the sea. Take a light spinning outfit and a reel carrying braid and you have a set up to allow for plenty of fun but little danger of being broken.

"As to why they take spinners, I'll let you decide. But if that sounds weird, woodlice have also worked, and some Devon anglers have even caught them on chips where fish are found in the vicinity of seaside takeaways."

It's perfectly true that thin-lipped mullet are a revelation on light spinning tackle, if you can hook the bastards. Quite why this mud-sifting machine should be stirred up by the pulse of a spinner is open to debate, but that flashing blade really gets them stirred up. If you've been sitting on a tidal river and growing old waiting for the tip to quiver, it's eye-opening stuff just watching one fish after another chase the lure. This is the easy bit, sadly. Many just follow to the bank, before they remember that they're mullet and not meant to be doing this sort of thing. Every so often however, a following fish comes forward, lips gobble and the magic begins. If you can shake off the idea that you're hallucinating, a quick strike will seal it. Thin-lipped mullet don't grow quite as big as the thick-lips, but you won't be worried about this when you're attached to one using light tackle.

The perfect territory for this specialist type of spinning is in a tidal river. Thin-lips travel quite far up estuaries, so you might find the best sport several miles up river as well as nearer the mouth. Finding them, as usual, is the easy part though and no method is guaranteed to catch mullet! That said, I can't remember the last time a session with spinners and worms failed to hook a fish or two.

Mullet will still test you. These fish follow almost lazily at times and the knack is in keeping a fish interested for several yards, but working the spinner slowly enough to let it take an easy bite. They rarely scoff hard, but will just mouth the worm. Baits with too much left dangling are a recipe for frustration, while even using a one-inch section of worm you need to strike instantly—whether you see the take directly or simply feel the fish pecking at the bait. It's vital to have a razor sharp, smallish hook and in a rocky, brackish setting I find myself sharpening hooks regularly.

As to why these take spinners in the first place, I'll let you decide. But if that sounds weird, woodlice have also worked, and some Devon anglers have even caught them on chips where fish are found in the vicinity of seaside takeaways. As for the spinner, the best theory I can come up with is that the blade represents a smaller fish, swimming along with a juicy worm it can't handle. Regardless of the truth, you won't care much when one of these striped fish fills the net, although you might wonder whether to kiss your catch or give it a slap in the face.

Is this the ultimate "pain-free" way of catching mullet? Probably not. But if my very life depended on catching one of these elegant, fickle bastards, I would be reaching for a box of spinners and a tub of worms. Just don't call them "British Bonefish", for Christ's sake. ●

River punk Aidan Curran
tackles the spooky trout of the Ara

A Suir thing

NO MATTER HOW MANY TIMES I PACK A SUITCASE OR STUDY THE GUIDE, fishing trips in far off places always sidestep expectations. From the picture you build in your head to the flies and even the weather, something different always hatches. Things mutate. Sometimes your best laid plans are lost in transit; other times you throw things together at the last minute but things just work. Sometimes you expect easy listening but you get punk rock.

Which is funny, because rather than some grand Irish River, this particular trip begins in a secondhand car in Tipperary. I hadn't been to Ireland for a good eight years, but the one picture I found reliably true to life was my host, Aidan Curran. A red-mohicaned punk with a taste for fly fishing.

"I guess I'm not your typical game angler," he chuckles, as the car rattles with loud music. No word of a lie. The bands we are listening to have names like SiCKPiG, Crisis and Runnin' Riot. "Pike fishing is definitely something that appeals to punks, but trout or fly fishing? It's not such an obvious match is it? People think you're pulling their leg."

Aidan's dented car takes innumerable turns down crooked country lanes as we seek out the river. Behind his own wild appearances is the subtler, laid back heart of an angler. In his own unique way, Aidan is just the next in a long line of colourful River Suir regulars, or should I say irregulars. Perhaps the greatest of them all was Liamy Farrell, depicted so beautifully in the writing of Niall Fallon, who describes a "rotund, stocky" bull of a man with "rolling, limping walk." Yet in spite of his burly frame and a rod that could have landed sharks, this grizzled character could make his fly land "like the kiss of an angel". He also knew the river better than anyone else, living and wading in it.

A refreshingly frank Suir angler from the present day is guide George McGrath, who meets us in stately-looking grounds by the Ara, a pretty little tributary of the Suir.

"Are you any good with a fly rod?" he asks, only half teasing. "Because if yer shite you won't be ketching much round here." With a slightly despairing shake of the head, George recalls an American guest with a PhD in entomology. A nice enough bloke with all the right gear who sadly couldn't hit the Rock of Cashel at 10 paces.

Quality water is abundant here, in fact the Suir and its tributaries offer the highest density of trout of any river in Ireland and quite possibly Europe. But that doesn't mean "easy" fishing, as George will testify. And he's fished these waters for so many years I'm wondering if his folks had a fly patch sewn onto his babygrow.

Lesson number one is in fly selection. The typical advice for Ireland is so often of the "big flies for big fish" variety and yet a peek at George's box reveals a good deal of specials in the size 16 bracket, with both little olives and sedges prominent. I need no second invitation to poach a few of these. The best river fishing begins quite late here, as late as June we're told, and perhaps the most prolific hatches are blue winged olives and various caddis.

Lesson two, about the legendary fussiness of local trout, is dispensed in the field as Aidan and I hop onto the Ara, a cute Suir tributary, for an initial foray. It looks beautiful in the sun. Shallow waters reveal trout by the dozen. They multiply before your eyes and are everywhere, flitting over the pale, sandy bottom of the river. You feel like you've stumbled upon paradise until you actually try casting for these little devils, which are among the spookiest trout I've ever come across in my entire sorry existence.

For the first two hours we try everything: long, fine leaders; tiny flies; longer casts. It's simply bordering on impossible to tempt these fish, or more precisely to get near them without raising panic. When I'd previously heard Aidan's missives about the shyness of the fish I had joked about him getting his hair dyed green instead of bright red. I now believe you'd need to be a camouflaged midget, invisible or able to levitate rather than wade to get anywhere near the buggers. It is pure agony to see such riches slip away at every bend in the stream.

Nevertheless, revenge is almost served as we have one final crack in a bigger bridge pool where a few more sizeable fish are lying and, touch wood, with more water to cover them don't seem quite so desperately spooky. With George joining Aidan on the bridge I now have two extra pairs of watchful eyes—and extra pressure!—to try and end a frustrating afternoon on a happy note.

"A little further upstream," or "Just in that hole, there!" come the regular words of advice. I can make out some shapes which are way bigger than the little runts we spooked earlier, but will they show any interest? The moment of truth comes as I manage to drop a heavy nymph so it passes right above a tempting little depression on the stream bed; a dark shape shifts across the current, there is a decisive flash and all hell breaks loose. For about five seconds the rod bends dangerously as I pay out line; next there is just slackness and a lone swearword. George's next declaration has already been ringing through my head: "He won't be coming back any time soon now."

WITH A WEEK OF SULTRY-HOT, DISTINCTLY UN-IRISH WEATHER AHEAD, most of our fishing the next two days takes place in conversations over coffee or beer. Trips to pretty local towns and crumbling relics appease our curiosity and also our womenfolk while we plot our next assault on the Suir. The history of the Irish regions is staggering but I'm relieved to find that the English are no longer seen as the number one bastards; that honour seems to be reserved for the current Irish government.

The area is full of ruins that, if they were in England, would have those bloody blue plaques everywhere and coachloads of invading pensioners. But here it is peacefully vacant. I admit to finding this slowly rusting side of Ireland reassuring. Samuel Beckett must have agreed when he wrote: "What constitutes the charm of our country, apart from its scant population, and this without help of the meanest contraceptive, is that all is derelict."

The bones of old castles sit splendidly idle, daisies growing from their windows.

Derelict beauty: The River Suir

Finally the Suir trout arrive, emboldened by the dusk

Such are the torn remains of what looks like a medieval turret sitting by the Suir just outside Cashel. The waters are sparkling and, as is always the case when you don't have a fishing rod, we spot trout moving in the stony runs and rushing water.

An evening return is plotted, but until that time we must content ourselves with fishing trips made in books. Among all the advice on Irish trout fishing are the accounts of night fishing such as those from Niall Fallon's *Fly Fishing for Irish Trout* are especially bewitching. On a hot summers' day this can be the only time Suir trout really drop their guard. The reasons involve science as well as alchemy; "invertebrate drift" is the term used to describe the nightly emergence of life forms on the river. During the witching hours, all that was hidden ventures out. An endless collection of creatures crawl from their hiding places on the river bed. The trout suddenly find their appetite and grow bolder.

This was also the favourite time of Liamy Farrell, who could be observed immersing his stocky frame into the river while more timid souls packed up for the evening. "Where others were glad to climb out of the strong waters of the Suir with an acceptable brace of trout on a July evening, Liamy would meet you on the bank in the warm, scented dusk with half a dozen, topped by a three-pounder" writes Fallon. "He liked to get right in amongst a shoal of feeding trout, moving with the utmost patience and slowness, and fish a very short line either side and above."

The first hour or two on our return to the Suir near Cashel begin with a friend of a friend and a rusty gate. The river drops away invitingly at the end of lush fields, but the only signs of life are odd rises well out into the current. Long leaders and distant casts earn only the most finicky of occasional takes until the light begins to fade. Aidan aims a team of traditional wet flies downstream to mix things up, but one hit and miss take is all our river punk can muster so far. Once again, we're foxed.

It is only as the light drops that the rises become more frequent and we spot a familiar, tall figure working the far bank. It is George, here to teach us a lesson presumably. Creeping along up to his thighs he searches the stony shallows with quick, short casts. Within minutes his rod jolts over and a Suir trout is kicking at his side. Aidan and I stand watching in that semi-appreciative way unsuccessful fishermen do in the presence of a local expert. Another trout comes to hand. And another the very next cast. "Just watch the bugger! You have to admit, he knows a trick or three though."

Hoping that the dying light will help to conceal my own lanky presence, I double back along the bank and drop into another shallow run, the water just about covering my knees. Where there was only a cool flow of water minutes earlier, there are now regular, splashy rises. As if someone had flicked a switch.

Tying on a small Balloon Caddis, I flick the fly into the stony run and pick up the line gingerly. I lose sight of the fly, but there is a sudden rush at the surface and I'm attached to a lively half-pounder.

Quite soon you can hardly make out the fly, but it hardly seems to matter. Numbers two and three follow, while the whole river seems to buzz into life. I throw a couple of painfully clumsy casts along with the better ones; the trout seem oblivious. At one stage they're rising directly just a couple of rod lengths behind me, totally untroubled.

Such is this magical time on the Suir that in the space of half an hour a frustrated amateur can be transformed into a trout fishing assassin. The change is so dramatic you wonder how you ever found it so difficult beforehand, but it's an exhilarating feeling. The fish don't sip, they smash. The best of them probably wouldn't trouble the pound mark, but they kick and thrash as hard as a punk rock band.

Tipperary is sleeping as we return home quite a lot later than planned, leaving the Suir to the trout and Liamy Farrell's ghost. Moths swarm down the overgrown lanes to Aidan's place as we gather in the night sky, still damp from the river. The best trout tastes beautiful, fried in butter. ●

Memories of Manhattan

HARLEM ON A SUNDAY AFTERNOON IS LIKE STEPPING INTO ANOTHER, MORE COLOURFUL WORLD. It might also be the last place on earth you would expect to catch fish, but appearances can be deceptive. On such days the upper half of Manhattan is transformed. The air is sweeter, the traffic slower. Even the capital of capitalism takes a catnap occasionally. The streets still bustle with activity, but of a different kind. The people stroll down the boulevards in their vibrant Sunday best. Many are church-bound, others just wander. Music floods the scene with the strains of rich, angelic gospel harmonies, the myriad voices, brass players and steel drums carrying sweet and true on the breeze, mingling with the dogs and the cars in an intoxicating symphony.

As I make the long walk from my dingy room on West 142nd Street down to Central Park the passers by don't quite know what to make of an Englishman carrying a fishing rod. Some smile, others just look quizzical. I idle past the brownstone terraces, the smallest of them four storeys high, counting down the street numbers. I pass men playing cards on the porch steps, enjoying a shady beer in the autumn sun. A one-handed chess player ponders his next move. I go down and down, reaching the edge of Spanish Harlem, pausing at a battered grocery store to buy a sandwich. The man in the store stops me, wants to know if there really are any fish in the middle of Manhattan. There are indeed, I assure him. He finds the idea most amusing. A friendly grey cat lounges on a drinks crate by the counter. The man offers to sell her to me for $10, an idea I find equally amusing.

I reach Central Park and the lake is bathed in golden, fall sunlight. It is a minor revelation just how green and calm it is here, such is the contrast between the peaceful "lungs" of Manhattan and her noisy, smelly innards. Harlem Meer, which must be several acres in size, may not be the most beautiful lake you've ever seen but has a charm all of its own. The trees are dwarfed by towering buildings beyond and yet it retains its peaceful isolation. Through its still, green surface the pointed, periscope heads of turtles emerge and if you listen beyond the muted bustle of the city you can hear the birds singing their own Sunday chorus.

One of the huge stones on the shore makes an ideal seat to fish from. Further along there are kids already fishing with cane poles and outsized floats, or "bobbers" as the Americans call them, which can be borrowed free of charge from the park rangers hut, complete with a pot of bread dough or sweetcorn for bait. A stocky, baseball-capped man is hurling out a gaudy red spinnerbait in the hope of bass. Further round the shore a smiling couple are fly fishing together. I tackle up my $30, pawn shop spinning rod, rig up and tie on a small hook. The "bobber" that clips onto the line, the smallest and least crude I could find, is red, white and bulbous, resembling something from a child's storybook. I mash up some bait to throw in and put corn on the hook. Soon enough the bobber starts to tremble. True to its name, it then bobs about playfully, before shooting ferociously out of sight. The rod rattles pleasingly and I bring in a pretty little bluegill, a fish which shares the spiny dorsal fin and bold biting characteristics of our perch, but with beautifully marbled cheeks; the perfect catch for a sunny afternoon in Manhattan.

More bluegills follow, joined by buttery-sided pumpkinseed sunfish of all sizes, novel and strange to my eyes, before I'm joined by unexpected guests. A little brother and sister sit behind me and start asking all manner of questions, as kids do. They find my accent plain weird and haven't a clue where England is. The boy starts casting his own bobber next to mine and I show him how to loose feed the swim to get more bites. I let the little girl take over my rod for a while and she giggles as the sunfish wriggle and jolt on the end of the line. The kids have no idea of the whereabouts of their mother, so I ask no more questions and we stick to talking about fish and fishing. The three of us sit there watching the bobbers and pointing at turtles, happy as the sunny lake itself, until they decide they should run off home.

A perfectly still evening follows. There is a curious pleasure in idly watching a float, enjoying a few lazy hours in the middle of one of the world's busiest cities. This is the ideal time to catch the modest largemouth bass that live here and I regret not bringing any spinners. Nevertheless, I manage to winkle out some colossal half-

Harlem Meer: a little surprise in the Big Apple

pound sunfish. The solitude never lasts long in Central Park however and I attract another random guest. This time it is a Finn who has lost his passport. I am guarded at first, but he seems friendly, well-travelled and speaks English more clearly than many of the New Yorkers I've met. We talk about Manhattan, Europe and the bloody-mindedness of US customs. He has nowhere to go, nothing to do but wait until he hears from the embassy and is grateful for the company. We take turns sipping a bottle of Finnish vodka and eating salt fish, which he assures me will do wonders for my health, until he too makes his way off. I wish him luck, but doubt he'll need it.

The perch-like bluegill, a common stateside catch

HIGH ABOVE CENTRAL PARK, ANOTHER LAZY FALL AFTERNOON AND MY MANHATTAN ADVENTURE TAKES ME TO THE VAST, TIDAL RIVER HUDSON. Creeping past the garages, warehouses and vacant lots of northwest Harlem you eventually reach the steely murk of this great waterway. Nestling amongst the run-down stores in this rusting corner of the island you'll even find some basic tackle shops. Whilst you might imagine that in America all the tackle is high tech, gimmicky and glamorous, there is quite a different reality here. The fishing shops I remember were gritty places, like converted garages. Fishy dens where the owners speak in broken English about fish like "porgies" and "stripers". On some premises the windows are so dirty the only way to find out if they're open is to try the door. These places sell all manner of paraphernalia, from basic rods and reels to bizarre lures and baits, all shrouded in a terminology quite alien to a Brit. At least I knew where I was with bait, and made sure I had a supply of "night crawlers", which looked suspiciously like lugworms, at my disposal.

Aside from the terminology of the sport, there is a language of fishing that is thankfully universal. Anglers everywhere are united by a shared enthusiasm, and casting out from a wall by the Hudson I found the people there friendly and helpful, if sometimes a little hard to understand. Most of the anglers lining up here are blue collar boys, Hispanic and African American labourers who man the garages and stores of the Upper West Side. They were curious about fishing in England, even though much of what I described was as unfamiliar as what they told me in return. Their world geography was appalling. One word I did understand was "bass", and one evening I watched a portly Hispanic man with a voice like grit wrestling with a big "striper" that scoffed his clam hookbait and must have weighed all of 6lb. At first all I could muster with my bastardised British shore

Small fish, big mouth: an urban bass

"At first all I could muster with my bastardised British shore fishing rigs were giant, blue-legged spider crabs; creepy, bizarre creatures, snatched straight from a horror film."

fishing rigs were giant, blue-legged spider crabs; creepy, bizarre creatures, snatched straight from a horror film, although I later discovered them on sale in the markets of Chinatown. I never did catch a monster fish from the Hudson, but the bass there were beautiful creatures, sleek and powerful with handsomely striped flanks.

The most charming and interesting character I met, however, was unlike most of the locals. He looked as out of place as I did and when we struck up a friendly conversation it transpired that he was a complete novice. This put us on an equal footing and we enjoyed our presence there as a pair of misplaced characters. His casting was dreadful, so I offered some tactful guidance. He revealed that he was a horn player by trade, playing Rat Pack songs in a Broadway show and wanted to take up fishing to unwind from the stress of constant rehearsals and performances. We talked about everything, from fast food to history and a shared love of jazz. Just as well, because in about three hours a small sea perch and a rather pathetic little bass were the sum total of our efforts.

Several years on I still wonder sometimes how Manhattan looks today, whether the bluegills are still biting in the park, whether the horn player ever learned to cast as elegantly as he spoke. Are the rusting corners, run-down stores and vacant lots still there up in Harlem, or have they given way to bland new developments?

On any adventure, sadly, the last cast is never far away. When my visa ran out it was hard to take my little black spinning rod back to the pawn shop. Cheap though it was, I had enjoyed using it and haggling over its value with strangers felt like a rather undignified end. With hindsight I now realise I should have given it to one of the kids down at the Meer in Central Park, but time was pressing and the dollars were running out.

So that was New York, at least for one English angler. A far cry from postcard visions of Time Square and Grand Central Station perhaps, but with travel, as with fishing, it is always the strange corners and unturned stones that interest me most. As far as angling experiences go however, fishing amidst five million people has to rank amongst the weirdest. ●

Happiness is a Pond

THE DELIGHT OF SKIVING SCHOOLBOYS AND AGEING MEN ALIKE, THERE IS SOMETHING MAGICAL ABOUT A SMALL, WEEDY POND. These are places where the usual rules of time don't apply; separate little worlds, where it is possible to forget about schools, offices, traffic or the bother that awaits on Monday morning. These are spiritual retreats for daydreamers, deadbeats and ramblers. If heaven exists, I imagine it to be a tree-lined pool where it is always summer.

For many of us, a local pond is the first place we ever cast a line. Most of those that I remember best start with a muddy track, the sort of road that belongs in a history lesson. In fact, an almost universal rule dictates that the worse the route you find, the more sublime the pond at the end of it. My own childhood favourite was such a place—where many adults would take one look at the gnarled, steep drive and think, "sod that". And for the five years or so I fished it, the ones who did make it up there would almost start the familiar tirade: "They really ought to do something about that track." I secretly hoped they wouldn't.

The route to Feneck Ponds must have been 300 yards or so of rutted stone and dirt on foot, but carrying too much tackle and desperate to reach the place, it always felt much further. And there were hazards too. Half way up were a trio of loud, deranged farm dogs, guardians of the track who threatened to take a chunk out of you, just for being there. And even when you'd seen them off it could be hot, steep work.

But what a place it was after the seemingly endless walk. The end of that beaten up track was like the threshold to another world. Through the trees it would suddenly emerge, perfectly still and pea green, fringed

by old trees and languid expanses of lilies. I couldn't hope to fish Redmire, the Avon or half the places I read about at the age of 13. But these ponds were tangible, yet similarly fantastic to my naïve imagination.

MOST BREATHTAKING OF ALL WAS GOING THERE EARLY IN THE MORNING, AT FIRST LIGHT. To our half-sleeping eyes the first pond resembled a huge bowl of soup, veiled in an intoxicating, eerie steam. The world seemed new again, fresh and alive. It was the best time of all to fish. We would hook roach, vivid green tench and best of all, if we were lucky, one of the pond's golden carp that would suddenly make your rod lurch and your heart race.

It was a fleeting little paradise, however. The mists would soon disperse as the sun rose higher, summer heat spreading lethargy over man and fish alike, the peace broken by the slamming of car doors as the regulars arrived to tackle up.

These ponds, scarcely covering an acre between them, were the scene for many happy summer days. Television bored me in the holidays and I was always far happier watching a red float tip, like a finely tuned aerial connecting me to the mysterious world below.

Books were one thing, but there are certain aspects of fishing you only learn through experience. With practice I could quickly sense the presence of a big fish in the shallow, green water. The fast plucks of

the tiddlers would die away as the water rippled with the motion of bigger fins. The little float would waver, before drawing under and away.

The battles were epic even if the fish, in hindsight, were not. As often as not, there would be a brush with the lilies, or a frantic few seconds of trying to wrestle a fish clear of tree roots. They still seemed

huge, probably because I didn't read the *Angling Times* at that age. The carp were beautiful creatures too; muscular, golden-scaled creatures that respected only calm persistence. Out of all of them, I best remember the great mirror carp my father once landed. At the time, its 10lb or so frame seemed spectacular, its glittering scales like 50 pence pieces.

The place became a regular pilgrimage for my brother and I, and for such a modest pond, it was brimming with secrets and signs. I still find it amazing how such bottomless mystery can exist in perhaps only half an acre of murky water. The element of surprise didn't end with fish either. A slightly mangy old hare quite often made his appearance, while grass

Happy returns: a crucian

snakes, frogs and swarms of tadpoles also loved the place.

We enjoyed it whether the fishing was good or indifferent and on slower days we would pass the time by catapulting blackberries or pieces of luncheon meat at each other. By lunchtime, when the sun blazed us into submission and the bigger fish were indifferent, we would fish idiot-style right under the bank and laugh at the microscopic carp and perfect little crucians that were there for the taking on pieces of sandwich. And there's the rub: my fishing might have become semi-serious in the decades that followed but I've probably never been any happier than those summer days.

WHERE HAVE THOSE TIMES AND THOSE PONDS DISAPPEARED I WONDER? At the same time we scaled that track in the early 90s, newer manmade lakes were already becoming big business as carp fever swept the country; heavily stocked, muddy holes where ambience was and still is a secondary consideration to catching scores of hungry fish. Weedy margins and wild flowers have been replaced by flat, manicured banks and easy access; quite a few have cafés, tackle shops and even portaloos to deny visitors the pleasure of pissing in hedgerows. The age of convenience fishing is upon us, it would seem, and even the owners of my favourite pond took note.

And that brings us to the million-dollar question: should you ever return, or is there wisdom in the words "never go back"? Is it possible, let alone advisable, to revisit those same banks and try to rekindle something? And how much of the experience is about our own innocence and imagination besides the waters themselves? Like returning to an old house or your first school, it can be a little strange and emotional.

I returned to Feneck Ponds one June to find a very different scene; levelled

Tomorrow's giant, at a hand's length

banks, wild grass mown flat, trees felled. It looked so much smaller too, as if the king-sized mystery it once held had been a mere illusion. They had even smoothed out many of the potholes in the track. Was this even the same pond? Had my memory tricked me? As far as I was concerned, they had converted the Garden of Eden into a garden centre. It was a bit like seeing your first love grow fat and cynical.

Fearing the worst, I stayed away for several years afterwards. It is only now, in fact, well into my 30s that I have been willing to take another look and tell myself not to be such a pessimist. After all, memory is a cheat and that golden past we dream of is a siren song to a place that only partially existed.

Feneck Ponds were still not the same, just as I am no longer the same. But nature is resilient and there are reasons for hope. The original trees may be gone forever, but the banks are lush and full again, sporting knee-length grass and wild flowers. This probably has more to do with a lack of management than any romance. Nevertheless, bubbles still emerge and the reeds move; the margins still swarm with tadpoles in the spring and if you hang around for long enough bats still skim the surface as night falls. I half-expected to see the old hare.

Best of all, you can still see the commotion among the lilies as a carp moves through and sucks noisily. Meanwhile, crucians nibble and although the monsters are unmoved by my bread today, I catch and gently return a tiny mirror carp no longer than my finger; a small symbol of hope that could grow to the size of a dinner plate given a few years. Life goes on for the creatures of the pool despite our intrusion, it seems, and I look forward to the day when the lane is a potholed disaster once again, when new trees flourish and the next generation fall under the deep spell of the pond. ●

a war of Worms

A WET CITY PARK ON A DAMP NIGHT MIGHT NOT SEEM THE MOST OBVIOUS SPOT FOR FISHING. But here in the damp turf are monsters. Not fish you understand, but lobworms of mutant proportions.

We are on the edge of winter. But there is no sign of frost, just rain. Wet grass, dark paths, random passersby.

It's a damp, close business, frankly. But there is a peculiar satisfaction in catching the bait you intend to catch fish with. Like

the actual process of fishing, you have to be prepared and lay aside your own comfort and convenience. And a dank, rain-drenched night is prime time for the biggest, juiciest worms. Which is why this evening all thoughts of being warm and dry like any normal human being are eclipsed by a different kind of logic, as I recall my grandfather's words: "The bigger the worm, the bigger the fish." As a 10-year-old boy this slogan had a beautifully simple logic as we ransacked the vegetable patch

for bait. Three decades later I still believe in the power of a big worm for a big perch. That's why you'll find me down at the park, when only teen smokers and lunatics are out, looking for a fresh supply.

As the rain picks up again the sodden park grows all but deserted. Just as well really, because it is an earthy process of bucket, dirt, hands and knees. Because it's only as you stoop down and really look that you start to find. Tails waver, bodies glisten. You might assume that grabbing a fistful of prime bait was a formality. Wrong.

Sometimes I actually think these specimen worms are harder to catch than the actual perch I want to tempt with them. Heads pop up suspiciously like little periscopes. One heavy step or clumsy move and they vanish in an instant. The trick is to move slowly within striking distance before grasping the worm with lightning speed. Some are gone before you know it. The rest must be eased out of the ground with a steady pull. Too much enthusiasm and you end up with half a worm. But with practice and persistence, you can amass two or three dozen before you risk being accosted by the local weirdo, or one of the neighbours notifies the local police.

THE ART OF PERCH FISHING ITSELF, IN SEMI-FLOODED DEVON AND SOMERSET, DOES NOT GET A LOT MORE GLAMOROUS. This is sport for the low season when the weather is moody and the days, like some of my friends, are short and brutal. Indeed, there is a certain time of year that defines perch fishing, but the timing is more down to necessity than romance.

Perch love crap, dull days when the light is poor. They don't really care if the rivers

Perch obsessive and high calorie operator Chris Lambert

are flooded, or it's so dark and miserable you can barely crawl out of bed. But the real miracle is just how well they thrive in some of the most unlikely settings: semi-derelict farm ponds, urban canals or muddy, soulless carp lakes conceal fish that defy their cramped existence. This is why winters are spent hopping between different ponds, following current leads and last year's rumours.

It tends to start with a new lake and an unrealistic optimism. My usual running mate is Chris Lambert, who crams his gear into my car while it is still dark. We'll stop at a random garage and I'll grab a coffee while he buys enough calories to feed an orphanage. Sausage rolls, crisps, Red Bull, the lot. And then it's roll-ups, cramped lanes and in today's case road closures as we negotiate the lanes around Bridgwater. My ageing van squeaks a little, The Stranglers rattle on the cassette player and Chris curses at the workmen telling us to turn round. It takes an age to find the fishery, but it's so dismal out there I almost prefer being cocooned in this car for the time being.

Viaduct Fishery is not exactly Redmire, to put it mildly. The lake we are looking for is one of a wet cluster of several, cut into the Somerset clay. A dirty yellow Robin Reliant sits there, stuck in the mud, as we fill in our names on cheap tickets like suspects. It's closer to sodding *Crimewatch* than Mr Crabtree, admittedly.

But if the start of today's fishery is rusty, the lakes themselves look promising. There are drowned branches and a stone "monk". Plenty of corners for a perch to hide too, but we're on autopilot since we've had a

Rusting machinery and another backyard perch lake

tip off on the lucky pegs, like numbers in a perch lottery.

So we set up and bait up as it starts to drizzle. I chop worms and Chris cuts prawns on a deep bank along the right side. But the fish don't bite. The breeze stiffens and the lake ripples, and for a few seconds I wonder what we're doing here. My pole sways in the wind and the sky darkens further.

For a little while, not a great deal is forthcoming. The first bite is not a sharp pull, but a gentle sinking of the float tip. A skimmer plods to the net and is returned with little gratitude as the rain starts to rip down and I mouth swearwords. For a few seconds I sit there and continue fishing, in a sort of state of denial, but it is no good. The maggots are crawling out of the bait tub, while various bits of tackle are hastily covered. Again, I wonder what possessed us to come here of all places on this day of all days.

Chris Lambert's shelter is a welcome little sanctuary as we look out over pocked water. Not one to mess about with poles or small baits, Chris is usually the polar opposite to me in the perch fishing stakes. Giant, raw prawns and live baits are his staple, along with industrial use of maggots and groundbait to draw in the prey fish. And while my greater finesse might draw more bites, he quite often emerges with the best perch of the day.

But for now, we are stranded and the world feels wet and useless. It hasn't even gone 11 o'clock but I decide to crack open the beer that was meant to celebrate a 2lb perch, while Chris lights a strange smelling roll-up.

"If a skimmer is like a fight with a vicar, a decent perch is like a punch up in a pub car park."

Eventually though, there is some degree of mercy and even a little afternoon sun. At one point it feels almost as if the day is starting afresh. The bites keep coming too, albeit from small silver fish, and after dropping in more chopped pieces of worm the float takes a walk, dips and there is a livelier fish attached.

The presence of a perch on light tackle is one of my favourite sensations in all of fishing. If a skimmer is like a fight with a vicar, a decent perch is like a punch up in a pub car park. The fish is still thrashing as it hits the net. It can't be much more than a pound, but on a shitty day these small victories are important.

For a brief spell the silver fish are gone and three similar-sized perch follow before the rain kicks up again. This is when your hope is really tested, when you reach for the biggest worm in the tin and dare something much larger to grab hold. But hope is a slag, and the only other drama is a bream, which for all of about five seconds convinces me it is a giant perch. And so today all talk of three pounders must remain just that.

MORE CRAMPED POOLS ARE FISHED OVER THE COURSE OF A LONG, WET WINTER, but few can be more measly than the elongated ditch we find just outside the village of Broadclyst, where a long time ago I once went to school. "Is this it?" asks Chris. "It's bloody tiny." Lying in front of us is an area you'd struggle to fit a game of five-a-side football, let alone a mixed fishery. Knotted brambles crowd the little pond, a weedy hole which can't be more than a third of an acre. Nevertheless, there's something irresistible about the backwater pool we meet.

How does a bit of water not much bigger than a tennis court hold such a mysterious pull? These are the sort of places you miss. They lie behind rusty gates, down farm tracks or tucked away where you least expect them. But in the internet age, it's refreshing for an adventure not to start with Uncle Google, but just a rumour, a hunch or a random glance through a car window.

Anything could be in here and finding out whether you've stumbled upon paradise or a pothole is all part of the fun. Today's little gem has no signposts or tacky fishing lodge. The stocks are a vague unknown, day tickets are "five quid, if I catch you," and the complete fishery rules list reads "Do Not Obstruct Gate".

If I'm honest we do know something about the fish stocks here; there are rumours of perch that defy the size of their home patch. The trouble is, the stories are so old that the Brothers Grimm might have written them. Secretly, I'm glad about this. Couldn't give a toss. I like the not knowing, truth be told.

Frost dusts the banks and our breaths hang like smoke, but a little sunshine is already poking through. We're meant to be perch chasing, but our maggots are quickly

met by hordes of little rudd. Even a juicy worm is fairly quickly annihilated. And so while I continue tiddler bashing, Chris lip hooks a fingerling rudd and flips it under a sheer, thorny bank.

Only as the mist clears do we receive a creeping run from a perch. The float pops and the line runs clean away as something solid grasps the rudd. But within seconds the hook pulls free and, for now at least, the corner of the pond remains an unsolved mystery.

All is still and clear for the rest of a perfectly cool morning that yields no further clues on the perch of this sleepy tarn. I can live with this while the spring sun is on my back, but things get restless, and Chris starts to run out of tobacco. I keep looking at the watch and get one of those terrible angler's hunches that nothing is about to happen for a very long time and about the best it'll get is a hot pie at the garage. In the end, I'm sort of unwilling to stay or leave. I start to count down a final 100 seconds and it is a single thought that detains me, the thought that somewhere in the black water under the brambles, lies a monster. Like a religious nut, I have no evidence beyond an out of date story, but I'm convinced it's true.

THERE MUST BE LITERALLY HUNDREDS OF PONDS IN MY HOME COUNTY OF DEVON ALONE, MANY OF WHICH HARDLY SHOW ON THE MAP. We are still in that early part of the year only a blind optimist would call spring, and our next Award-Winning Fishery is first glimpsed through clustered snowdrops and rusting farm machinery. A sheltered area catches the eye, with snags and deep holes that all whisper perch. Big carp and roach are also alleged residents, but the only facts the two other anglers present can agree on are that the weather is unseasonably warm and the owner is mad.

Chopped worms are dropped down the sloping shelf on the deep end of the lake where we set up. The fine bristle of a pole float sits crisp on the water. Everything looks textbook, in fact, but the only early response is from aggressive little perch that look too small to have any right to grab a lobworm. Meanwhile, Chris snatches tiny roach on float tackle in search of a few perch baits.

Contrary to the usual angling rulebook, the fishing improves beyond all measure as the sun gets higher and the sky clears. Bigger perch begin to bully away the little ones, and in these circumstances I am always happy to really pile the chopped

A monster perch from a modest pool

worm into my swim, or to "Bob Nudd the shit out of it," in Chris Lambert speak.

The next barely slips the float tip under, before the centrepin creaks and spills line. For the first time in a while, I am playing a perch with a genuine nervous excitement. Ironically, in perch fishing, the clearest sign you have a big one from a stillwater is the laziness of the fight. Even so, the relief is palpable as the net is sunk and I unhook a brute of a perch that looks so hunch-backed, mean and overgrown it must have been in the pond since the 1980s. No other fish has that strangely lovable menace of a big perch.

Bites continue in no set order, but the better fish quite often give little more than a sly dip on the float tip. It never ceases to amaze me how a fish so formidably equipped in the gob department can give such shy takes. Exactly why the perch won't readily accept a small prey fish is perplexing, our own theories as muddy as the water itself.

I can't manage any improvement on the fish that comfortably dwarfs the others, but by the late afternoon we have amassed some fine perch between us. Just to add a further twist as we decide to free them all from the keepnet, Chris is convinced that the biggest perch in the keepnet has "got fatter". At first I'm sceptical, wondering if a little hole in the net might account for the odd missing tiddler. But when he dares me to re-weigh the fattest of the perch, it has grown by three ounces. It would be a bit of a cheat to claim this new weight, we both agree, but regardless of the figures we have finally stumbled upon that great day of perch fishing that didn't end in wet disappointment or bream slime. And as for the value of the worms, the evidence is written all over my filthy fingers. ●

This aint no Chalkstream

Pretty but cramped territory in the way out west

FOR ALMOST ANY ANGLER, THE IDYLLS OF THE SPORT ARE A VERY DIFFERENT REALM TO A WET SUNDAY AFTERNOON. But it is in the often well-heeled world of game fishing that the gulf between fact and fiction can be starkest of all. There still exists, at least in the popular mind, a sort of fly fishing nirvana populated by the upper crust. For these happy few, life is about carefully maintained decorum and equally well-maintained chalkstreams, far away from the hoi polloi and their muddy ditches. We imagine smooth, open glides of water, where traditional flies tempt big, flawless trout; a place where men still sport waxed facial hair, smoke pipes and speak openly about the virtues of the Greenwell's Glory or Wickham's Fancy without blushing.

The world I am talking about is, of course, largely a work of fiction, a place that may as well be Middle Earth. Perhaps that's because this sacred realm of idyllic yet elitist tradition scarcely really exists any longer. In truth the exclusive beats of today are populated by more banking executives than retired colonels, complete with 3lb trout born on fish farms. Not that I rub shoulders with many business executives, you understand. Indeed, I have spent much of my life with coarse anglers. Some very coarse anglers, to be precise. The sorts of characters I usually encounter on the bank smoke Superkings rather than pipes and prefer tracksuits to tweed. Naturally, I'm trying to do something about this. Trouble is, I am currently as short on well-connected friends as I am on hard currency. A syndicate ticket on the Test, for example, would probably require me to sell an organ.

The fact of the matter is that my own fly fishing career has not so much been a tale of sunny chalk streams and mayflies, but muddy tracks, biting insects and barbed wire fences. But there's something magical and unexpected about wading a craggy stream where nobody goes.

THE FIRST RULE OF THE GAME IS SIMPLY TO FIND YOUR OWN AFFORDABLY WILD RIVER. It may sound easy, but some parts of the Amazon basin see more visitors than the places I frequent. A friend of a friend's old man happens to be a farmer who happens to have a stream on his land which he lets the odd angler try for a fiver on rare occasions. Convenience fishing it isn't. No cosy swims or easy parking here. Unspoiled, I sometimes say, by which I mean bordering on unfishable.

A high summer's day is perhaps the most risky and promising time of all to explore this rough and ready school of stream fishing, on today's random river. Today's mile or so walk, having parked next to a pile of dead tyres is not altogether unexpected. Crossing the edge of a firing range is slightly more, shall we say, unscripted. I already have my suspicions about the colourful little cases littered around, before a shot rings out. Before I can be misidentified as a poacher I make my way swiftly off in the other direction. After all, fly fishing is a sport best enjoyed without being riddled with gunshot.

Although much appreciative of still being alive, the river itself is sadly missing. I must have read thousands of words on finding fish, but nobody to my mind has ever covered what to do if you can't actually find the water. *The Compleat Angler* has no mention of wire fences and shotgun shells. As far as I remember, Walton's England was one of meadows and milkmaids, not

"Charles Cotton definitely never said to Walton 'So Izaak, where's this sodding river you keep banging on about?'"

pathetically cramped streams owned by UKIP voters. Charles Cotton definitely never said to Walton: "So Izaak, where's this sodding river you keep banging on about?" Which brings me to rule number two in the budget fly fisherman's handbook: never trust any directions that end in the words "you can't miss it".

After one or two branches in the face there is the river, finally. And worth every step. I simply love small, wild streams where there are no Sunday anglers or stocked fish. No local know-it-alls or formbook to study. Just a meandering little brook stuffed with wily little trout. Of course, you do have to get into the water first, which can be no mean feat.

The obligatory barbed wire fence comes first. As if set to some heinous formula, these vicious obstacles have a nasty habit of being too high to climb over, yet too low to go crawling underneath. Somehow, I get over without putting holes in my waders or becoming a soprano singer. Then, for my next trick, comes the descent into the drink. I find a convenient gap, where there is a mere six foot drop into the water. It's a feat I manage with little grace; a heavy man plunging into the water size 14s first has obvious consequences on a little river—every fish for about half a mile spooks.

But as soon as I am wading and casting, the day quickly gets better. Not easy, but better. A world away from a big, well-coppiced river, these surroundings are more like a scene from Conrad's *Heart of Darkness*. It's somewhat tight here to say the least, a maddening blend of fishy-looking corners and intervening branches and snags.

But it's this trickiness that is addictive. It is a mixture of luck as well as skill, flipping low casts into shady water, extracting trout from the stones and catching your flies in trees. Wading, watching, cursing, chancing and just occasionally winning.

The art of the impossible cast has a particularly fatal draw for me. A hair's breadth can divide victory from certain death and I've probably lost more flies than a fire at Fulling Mill. Today it is sod's law that the most spectacularly craggy little

Worth the gamble: a spectacularly wild trout

corner is the fishiest-looking of the lot. Tell tale rings emerge from the trout rising from within their little sanctuary. To say that behind me there is little space would be a crude understatement; if the branches on one side didn't look good, the other bank is a totally choked with Himalayan balsam.

Inch by inch I creep smartly, ever so carefully into position. One step too few and my cast will find the trees and assorted godless, tangled things behind; one step too far and those keen-sighted trout are sure to bolt.

The first cast catches the foliage behind me. I let out a hushed profanity as I pull at the line. Luckily the fly drops free. I wait anxiously for some moments, watching to see if the fish are still rising after this clumsy first serve. This time, to my own disbelief, I guide my little dry fly slap bang on the money, just under the branches. Almost immediately there is a little sip and I lift instinctively, feeling the pulse and arch of the rod.

There is nothing wilder looking than one of these bush trout, riddled with spots and smooth as stone. As I release the fish, I'm fairly certain this will be the first and last time anybody bothers it, which is perhaps as it should be.

This is why I tramp through miles of undergrowth, duck fences and risk silly casts in lost corners. This is why we all do it, put up with the inconvenience, the expense, the frustration. To remind ourselves that there are still wild places where nobody goes. To feel as if, successful or otherwise, you are the only sucker who exists for a few hours. As for the chalkstream? You can keep it. ●

OF ALL THE SETTINGS FOR AN ALIEN INVASION THEMED B-MOVIE, TORQUAY SEEMS ODDLY APPROPRIATE. The very heart of this seaward facing town presents a curious mixture of the everyday and the outlandish. Palm trees sway above hedgerows; crumbling terraces sulk between the opulence of 5-star hotels and glitzy gambling halls. As the summer heat arrives the entire sea front is awash with lights, gaudy neons blurring with yellows and whites. But it isn't just the tourists who find themselves hypnotised by the glow.

Along the harbour's outer wall, eerie shapes loom and throb. As the daytime crowds depart, the water stirs with oozing, tentacled ghosts. It is no fantasy or trick of the light, but visiting legions of squid. Like the revellers along the bars of the sea front, they are drawn towards the lights in search of fast food and the opposite sex. Jetting around in sinister fashion their suckered arms stick fast to prey such as prawns and small fish—which are then devoured by a sharp, chitinous beak.

Awash with bizarre interlocking and fairly indescribable body parts, the sex life of the squid is scarcely any less weird, but the milky clusters of eggs sticking to the traps and mooring ropes in the harbour tell their own story. It's a lifestyle even Torquay's stranger residents couldn't rival. Thankfully, the process of catching them is less complex, although equally fascinating.

A hot spring evening on a rising tide is prime time for the curious business of "squidding". As the sun sinks across the bay, lights flicker to life all along the harbour throwing pools of yellow light into the shady hollow of the wall below. You sense that anything could turn up at this magical time of day. Beneath the walkway a cuttlefish trembles its way along the stonework, just under the surface. Moments later I wonder if I'm seeing things as a hundred-strong procession of pale mullet cruise past our position.

In spite of these strange distractions I keep my focus on the squid. Absent are the usual tools of the shore angler's trade. A pink squid jig with a double crown of fine hooks is the weapon of choice here. Regular doses of torch light help to give it a luminous charge, which should help our tentacled killers find it. Some locals present this under a float, but I decide to start by fishing it like a lure, with a drilled bullet for a little extra casting weight.

*"Along the harbour's outer wall,
eerie shapes loom and throb."*

Strange means: a special jig with more points than a pincushion

CASTING INTO THE GLOOM IS EXCITING STUFF, JUST THE PLOP OF THE JIG LANDING GIVING AWAY ITS PRESENCE. Drawing it back in a series of little glides the jig cuts an odd, gleaming form beneath the surface. Small fish dart out from under the wall to investigate this Chernobyl-style lure—but where are the squid?

As the darkness gets heavier—I'm tempted to say "inky"—the answer arrives in sudden fashion. Just beyond the glow of the lights something engulfs the lure in its lashing arms. The rod begins to bend with a strange presence. The fight is a curious oozing, pulsating power unlike any fish. But before I can catch sight of the thing below, the pressure disappears just as abruptly. Hanging on the jig however is the first piece of grisly evidence itself—the rubbery, torn off end of a tentacle! Squid fishing lesson number one is duly noted—keep the pressure at all times and draw your catch in as steadily and quickly as possible.

As jigs are hastily revitalised with the aid of a torch, hopes are lifted by further oddities stirring beneath the wall; shimmering white freaks moving in spurts and starts—monsters that wouldn't look out of place attacking Captain Nemo's submarine, never mind buggering about in Torquay. Their translucent colours serve as a shifting camouflage which conceals them from both prey and enemies.

With a slight shudder, the jig returns to the water to sink slowly amidst the night waves. A few turns of the reel and another sinister embrace is made. This time the squid is better hooked. It writhes against the pressure for a few tense moments before I bring it up and into the light.

I'm about to handle the catch but have second thoughts when it spits out a jet of oily black ink. A quick trip to the ice bucket quickly pacifies the creature—and I'm told is the kindest and least messy way to proceed. Cast aside the alien looks of these creatures and they make excellent eating.

A tantalising hit and miss game of jigging continues into the night as the squid continue to move in. Besides regular recharging of lures by torchlight, I also experiment with a battery-powered night float with the aim of drawing the squid closer. More bites, or should I say grabs, are experienced. More often than not the squid seem to come adrift. Cuttlefish also lurk close to the wall but these equally alien visitors prove surprisingly shy when cast to.

It's also fascinating stuff just quizzing the locals and my knowledge of squid grows tenfold in the course of an intriguing few hours. I'm told the squid can be found here en masse if you get your timing right—

Finally an invader is landed, albeit by a mere tentacle

but a few are present all through the summer. This also seems to explain many of the slow, deliberate bites you get here on fish or prawn baits which materialise into nothing. These creatures have a short life cycle, usually only two to three years, but grow quickly and the biggest can be expected later in the season. An explosion of baby squid in the summer perhaps also explains why the small ones can make good baits for bass here.

Whether you keep a few for bait or to eat, it makes sense to take a good-sized bucket or cool bag with plenty of ice. It's a rewarding diversion in more ways than one, as well as one of the weirdest angling trips you'll ever make. It's fishing Jim, but not as we know it. ●

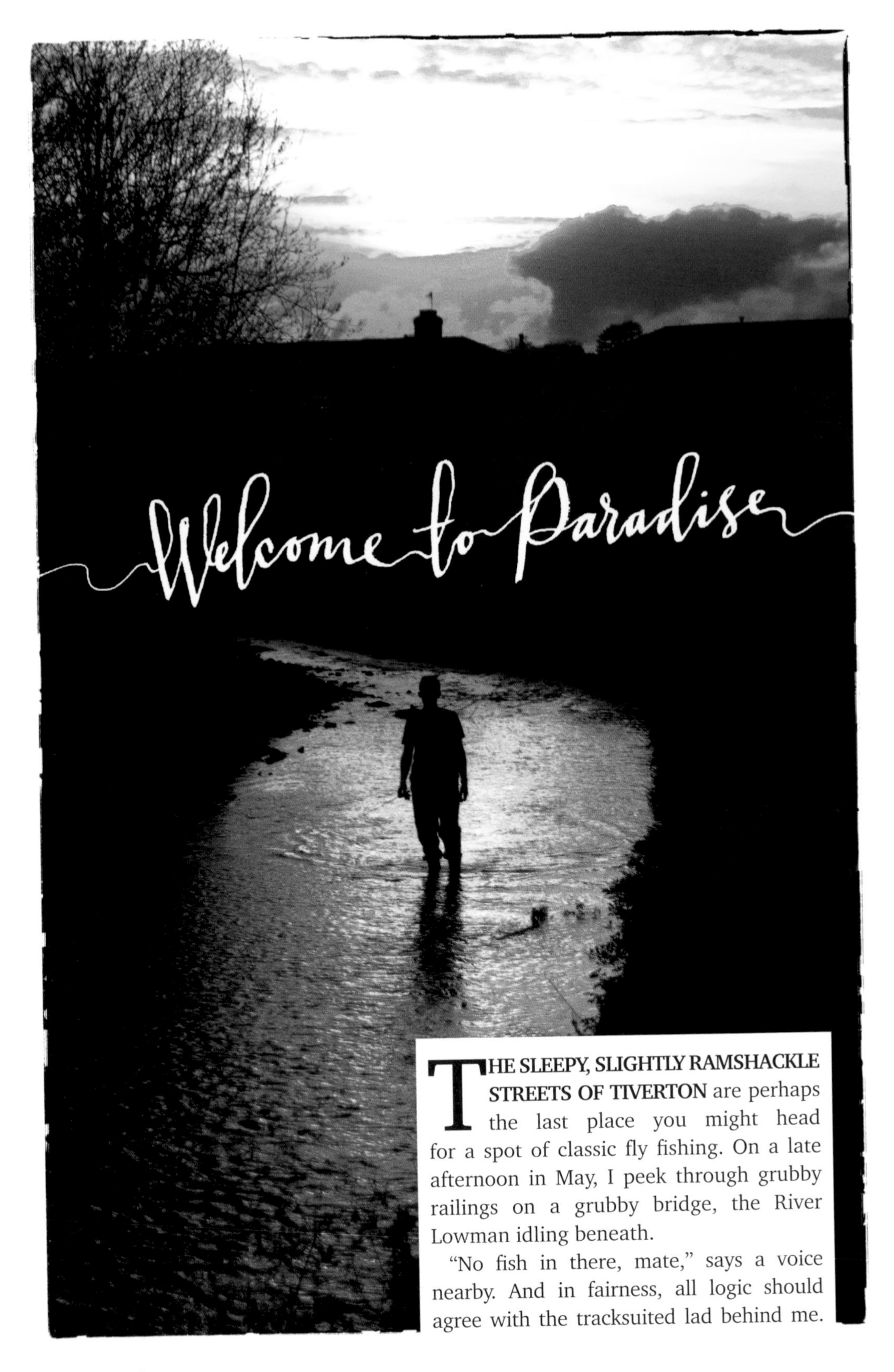

THE SLEEPY, SLIGHTLY RAMSHACKLE STREETS OF TIVERTON are perhaps the last place you might head for a spot of classic fly fishing. On a late afternoon in May, I peek through grubby railings on a grubby bridge, the River Lowman idling beneath.

"No fish in there, mate," says a voice nearby. And in fairness, all logic should agree with the tracksuited lad behind me.

Mid-stream, you can make out what looks like a radiator, flanked by a carrier bag and fragments of broken pottery. But there is more here than just random wreckage. As the stream deepens, there is a flicker of life over the stones. I scan the streambed for a few seconds only half believing, the rock hues and shadows blurring as I spot a flicker of movement. Seconds later, I see him clearly: A foot-long trout, wildly spotted but easy to miss. The fish edges across the flow before holding position, seemingly untroubled by the procession of bodies passing overhead.

You do wonder what such a wild creature is doing, swimming under cramped streets and the diesel thrum of buses. But besides litter, there's life in the stones. Just upstream, a small, pale mayfly emerges. A second then appears on the wing. A few moments later comes the moment of truth itself: a juicy, definite rise. As the rings at the surface gently subside I begin to feel like less of an idiot carrying a little trout rod through this urban sprawl.

I find an access point down a little slipway further on. Wading gently along, I find the water surprisingly clean. There is a fair clarity over the sandy brown stones. With the odd empty tinnie also on display I am tempted to describe it as beer-coloured.

I stalk carefully into position and try to pretend this is just a usual little trout stream like any other, but it proves difficult. With a small audience already forming on the bridge I feel like some obscure street entertainer, as I make a cast into the run ahead.

By cast number six there are schoolboys at the railings, watching me watch the trout. I'm issued a challenge: "Oi mate, what you doing? You won't catch anything." I don't say anything but find the perfect response, as the fly lands on a little sill of water and is neatly grabbed by a rising trout. There is a little flash of opening mouth before the little brook rod lurches round to a near semicircle, as connection is made with my first Tiverton trout, no more than a double haul from the bus stop. It is no giant, but a vividly marked trout, which kicks and turns well for its size. The schoolboys are impressed, regardless, demanding a look before I slip the unlucky thing back to go and swim with the empties and the radiator.

IN A LITTLE POOL FESTOONED WITH DEBRIS, TROUT BEGIN TO MULTIPLY, MUCH TO MY SURPRISE. One by one they emerge from the stones, suddenly visible in motion. They are hungry fish too. A small Hare's Ear attached New Zealand-style under the dry proves their undoing, and I earn another hat-trick of brownies in this one run alone, missing many other bites in the process. For a few happily oblivious minutes I could be fishing a favourite wild brook some 20 miles away, not a care in the world. Until, that is, I look round to find that like the trout, the schoolboys and assorted onlookers have multiplied into a full rogue's gallery at the railings, drawn by the rather surreal sight of a fly caster in motion in the concrete heart of the town.

I soon decide to move on in search of somewhat more secluded urban fishing, if that's possible. The boys offer some local advice as I get out of the river and back onto the street. I let one or two of them try my polarising glasses to spot a few well-concealed town trout for themselves, a game which they enjoy. The next thing I'm told, however, makes me wonder whether the whole episode is just a bizarre dream. "Keep walking that way, and you'll get to Paradise." Are they serious? You have got

Fly fishing is anything but private in Tiverton

to be shitting me. The concrete bordered stream filtering off ahead looks about a million miles away from any kind of paradise you could imagine. They mean Paradise Fields, an area of playing turf and footpaths well known to these local lads; a place where the trout swim by the dozen and are all two feet long, according to my new friends at least. It sounds too good to be true while you pass the local scrapyard and random acts of fly tipping, but I'm as enthusiastic as any schoolboy when it comes to fishing talk.

PERHAPS HALF A MILE ON WE APPROACH PARADIS. Past a skateboard ramp and local football pitches, you can trace the line of the stream, an Exe tributary, that still runs clear and true in spite of the vast Tesco nearby and the brickwork of manifold small businesses. With a series of little pools, runs and distinct "steps", it is not altogether unattractive. If you squint in places you might even imagine what this lively water way was like before modern development—a happy little stream, full of life. With eyes open wider however, you can't help feeling a little saddened by the litter and signs of casual disregard evident here. A long list of debris includes plastic bags and bottles, a spanner, cans, plastic toys, sacking and the obligatory shopping trolley. Mid-stream further on is a rusty bicycle, poking up defiantly against the flow. Unperturbed, I send loops of fly line out over the flowing water, whilst in a nearby car park, two workers on a fag break ponder whether I've lost my marbles.

I may appear a touch eccentric, but this urban brook is not merely a tale of debris and depression. In the shallows I turn stones to uncover various nymphs, from baetis to cased caddis. And while the area is not exactly rife with invertebrates, I have sampled more secluded rivers with a great deal less happening down below. Luckily enough for our own careless species, nature is resilient, sometimes surprisingly so. Some of these Devon streams would once run strange colours as the printers leaked dye into the river. But with the decline of industry, many of these urban rivers are reawakening. This little Paradise, in name at least, proves not to be short of a trout or two either.

The broken and undecided sky keeps allowing a hopeful sun through onto the running water, where I can already pick out a dark-backed fish. It is a tricky game to avoid

A long list of debris includes plastic bags and bottles, a spanner, cans, plastic toys, sacking and the obligatory shopping trolley. Mid stream further on is a rusty bicycle, poking up defiantly against the flow.

spooking these Paradise trout, which are keen-eyed and quick to take flight, in spite of their assumed familiarity with people. The odd splash of a football crashing into the water from a nearby training session doesn't exactly help either, but I guess that in this crowded modern world Paradise is something that must be shared.

With my tall frame looming all too high over the low, clear water I resort to stooping, kneeling and even crawling into position on each little run. On several occasions I curse quietly at the sight of sleek, dark forms shooting away from me. Pretty shy for urban trout, these Tiverton brownies. Slowly but surely though, I proceed carefully and get my opportunities. Each little run comes to a head of stronger, more intense flow and a nymph dropped into the corners here, where hectic and calmer water meet, is quickly snaffled. Each time the fight is a punchy, pulsating affair with my little brook rod, resulting in another startlingly healthy little trout, each with beautiful hues of copper, brass and butter.

Pushing on further into Paradise, the stream grows leafier, if still distinctly urban. As I proceed under a graffiti-spattered road bridge, something kisses the water ahead, another tempting sign of life. The current hurries along here around a tight little corner to form an obvious focal point. Try as I might however, my flies are ignored and the only interest garnered is that of a group of perhaps a dozen local teens, a ragtag bunch of bored-looking boys and girls simply hanging about. After some minor apprehension, a simple "hello" is all it takes for them to drop their guard. The lads in particular are curious about the fly tackle and offer me their own thoughts on catching trout, mostly with worms and spinners. The ringleader and his mate examine the flies in my box with naive fascination. One or two of the younger ones climb a tree just ahead and soon put down any nearby trout, but I'm not troubled by this. In spite of all the negative media and scare mongering about "broken Britain" and its youth, it strikes me that these youngsters are not bad kids, just bored kids, perfectly

"under a graffiti-spattered
road bridge, something kisses
the water ahead"

These "townie" trout are just as wild as their rural cousins

affable if you respect them. Their language might not always be pretty, but give them just a minute or two of your time and they are naturally curious about trying to catch trout on a fly, about the casting, about nature here and the river itself. And unlike adults they are refreshingly unreserved. Amongst various random questions I get a real mixed bag of conflicting advice, recommended spots and silly jokes in the space of a few minutes, before I part with these unlikely fly fishing students.

With an increasing amount of foliage, I begin to catch more trees than trout, even with a short brook rod as my weapon of choice. As you gain some distance on the town centre in these reaches, the terrain becomes an even stranger mismatch of town and country. A fluttering sedge dances as the light fades somewhat, but I fail miserably to get into position in a tempting but impossibly overgrown swim. Overhead on the far bank loom strange stacks of metal and plastic waste, crushed into blocks, some of which were once cars. And yet when you keep your eyes on the stream, it is strangely and defiantly wild here.

As evening draws in, the sun begins to dip on this unlikely paradise. Street lamps flicker on and the shadows lengthen. The surrounding outlines are a strange cocktail of organic and manmade forms, from the many rooftops of new houses with their jagged aerials to swaying trees and the immovable curves of the hills beyond. Is this what the future looks like? As I stroll back to the town the final whistle is blown on the playing fields and the footballers are quietly leaving the field. The calming sound of the stream slowly blurs with and then gives way to the low hum of traffic. On the fringes of the grass there are flowers amongst the litter. There is beauty beyond the dross, but only if you are prepared to look. Perhaps there is hope yet for the little stream? ●

Hangover Blues

I GUESS YOU COULD SAY I'M A DRINKER WITH AN ANGLING PROBLEM, RATHER THAN THE OTHER WAY ROUND. Both habits have their price, but fishing is the fiercer addiction. Rain, raging winds or illness rarely stop me. Certainly not a lousy hangover. But there are hangovers and then there are hangovers. And this one fell into the latter camp.

You know you were drinking hard the night before when you have to use the walls to negotiate your way to the bathroom sink. It's a mystery to me how so much "refreshment" can leave anyone

so violently thirsty in the morning. Your pounding head feels as if it has been crushed into a different shape, your body the subject of some cruel and meaningless experiment. You only went to sleep five hours ago. Sane members of the human race find a quiet corner to curl up and die peacefully, but not you. No, because the new trout fishing season opens today and your brother is threatening to pick you up in 10 minutes, hopefully in a more sober state than you are. It'll be relaxing, you tell yourself. It'll take your mind off your pounding head and empty wallet, you tell

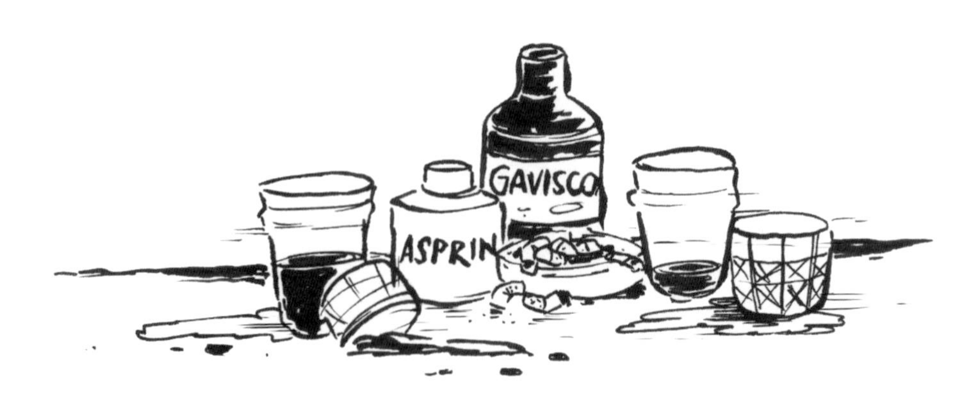

yourself. Fat chance, says the portion of your brain that isn't still pissed.

I'm barely dressed by the time the doorbell rings. After a quick cup of tea accompanied by toast and aspirin, we hit the road. Just what a hangover victim needs; an hour's drive on crooked country roads. For the whole journey big brother talks up the new season, whilst I'm focused less on textbook fly fishing techniques than the more pressing issue of holding down my stomach contents. Over every dip and bump I curse the local councils whose road building skills seem stuck in the 17th century.

Finally, the river is there and like the last Pope, I almost want to kiss the ground as I stumble out of the car. I am now demonstrating second phase hangover symptoms. Everything seems immensely funny. From the complete lack of visible insect life on the river to the fact that we just passed a village called "Broadwoodwidger," it's all, quite frankly, bloody hilarious. I try to suppress the sniggers. My brother just shakes his head knowingly.

A BITING WIND SOON WIPES THE SMILE OFF MY FACE AND THE ONLY SALVATION LIES IN CASTING OUT A LINE, which is accomplished with surprising efficiency given my condition. The rhythm of casting provides a calming distraction from the sickness and, quite unexpectedly, for a brief few minutes all is golden. The sun peeps through the clouds warming my back, the river looks beautiful and for a lingering few moments I forget all about my wretched state. I could be dying and still enjoy wading in this pretty stream. Not a fin stirs around my fly, but I don't care too much as my very soul feels as if it's thawing out in the sun.

It lasts perhaps 15 minutes before the north wind arrives, bringing hail with stinging, spiteful wind. The day turns out to be a real mess of different weather, from sunshine to sleet, the only constant being the relentless wind which numbs the fingers and makes mending the line a pain rather than a pleasure.

I keep fishing through it all, hours passing without a touch, wondering if the trout are also hungover and telling myself over and over that in my present state the only thing worse than fishing is not fishing. I try to concentrate on the remedy rather than the sickness, but it gets to a point where any optimism is waning and a switch must be made.

Plan C is the dreaded indicator and heavy nymph combination. I convince myself that surely on this cold spring day the fish are lying lethargically on the river bed, like last night's revellers perhaps, and will only respond to something put right on their noses. I pass over all the realistic fly patterns in the box in favour of a gaudy orange bug, expecting nothing of it. It is a true hangover creation, possibly from a previous weekend's aftermath, the sort of fly tied on a whim from the materials you

"My fingers get so numb I can hardly knot a fly of any description and there is no denying it, I need my bed. My bed and possibly a minister."

never use, just for the sake of something to do on a wet Sunday in the closed season.

The next slower stretch I come to seems ideal, slower and deeper, as I run my somewhat ridiculous bug through it. Not as deep as I thought, as the indicator drags under. But to my astonishment, it is not the bottom I then feel but a jagging weight pulling away.

There is a wallow of drunken silver in the river. It is no trout, but a perfect grayling that looks equally surprised at our unlikely meeting.

Once again, the hangover is forgotten for a few glorious minutes as I gently return this out of season but very welcome guest. Slightly further up the run and exactly the same happens—a bigger grayling, just shy of a pound this time, puts another pleasing curve in the rod. But my lucky brace of grayling bring a new problem. Rather than an early return home to recover, my older brother is now unwilling to call it a day.

I'd be lying if I said the rest of the day was a pleasure. I'd be lying if I said it was "character building" or that it taught me a lesson. I keep my urging stomach in check and my mouth closed. I have a violent thirst and a bad head. Not for the first time, I consider with regret the rotgut combination of booze that has been my undoing: vile spirits and dodgy local ales, another evening of basic common sense pissed up a wall. The government could probably use me as some sort of health warning.

I keep fishing through the hangover almost like an alcoholic stays on the lash; out of need rather than for fun. It is pure endurance for the most part. I discover a new leak in my waders and wish I'd worn another layer. To make matters worse, the inevitable happens when the bizarre orange fly finds a tree and my confidence disappears with it.

My fingers get so numb I can hardly knot on another fly of any description and there is no denying it, I need my bed. My bed and possibly a minister. I close my eyes and try to focus on the soothing sound of the river, but the only rhythm that gets through is the pounding inside my head. I keep praying that a fish, one of any description, will hang itself on my brother's nymph so we can go home. He too takes an untimely grayling but in typical big brotherly fashion feels he has to at least equal my count of two fish. After all, who wants to be beaten by their hungover younger brother?

Rather than my pleas for mercy it is only the foulest possible weather that eventually persuades Ben to stop fishing and drive us home. In the end you'd have to say that stinging hail is a better argument than any I could come up with.

I'm pleased to report that I haven't had a hangover like it since. In fact I'm laying right off the drink. The fishing, on the other hand, is one antisocial habit that I am not about to kick. ●

walker's lost pool

YOU MIGHT EASILY MISS IT FROM THE MAIN ROAD. A glance at neighboring industrial units and the rumble of heavy machinery and you might easily wonder if the place ever existed. A classic-looking carp lake, amid the dust and the din of a busy quarry on a main road?

It starts with a layby and a bare-bones gate. And then you spot it. Guarded by tall, wiry trees is the stillness of an old pool. These sleepy few acres of water may not look like much today, but in the early days of carp fishing, eyes widened at tales of monsters patrolling this quiet, flooded clay pit.

Dick Walker and Jack Hilton were just two of those captivated by the place. The possibility of a 30lb carp fuelled long haul visits and sleepless nights. Plans were made and unmade, strange baits were tossed into the lilies.

THERE IS ALWAYS A DANGER IN SEARCHING FOR LOST TREASURE. Does anywhere ever remain pure, unchanged? Sometimes the search for fishing paradise takes you to an industrial estate. But perhaps the fact that it still merely exists is enough, because Abrook Pond is still beautiful in its own way. As we walk the perimeter of the water, birdsong mingles with the sound of drilling. Mercifully enough, many of the trees have been left; craggy survivors which were scaled by visiting carp spotters back in the 60s. And here I am, half a century late to the party, scratching for clues.

If I learned one lesson from the tattered copy of Dick Walker's classic *Stillwater Angling* I read as a teenager, it was the importance of a good recce in search of the fish. And so I forgo bait and rigs and start with my feet. A little wooden bridge leads us to the far bank, a journey revealing clusters of lilies and mating damselflies. Dark shapes cruise beneath bushy overhangs; rubbery lips "cloop" in the weed.

However modern fishing becomes, the actual fish change little over time. These carp are as cunning and secretive as ever. The handful of giants that inspired earlier visitors are gone, but the fish still run to around 20lbs here. The tackle used to catch them, however, is scarcely recognizable. Cane rods have been replaced by carbon fibre and bite alarms.

Thoughts of high-tech rigs and spodded boilies cross my mind briefly as I look across the pond, but such tactics seem like sacrilege. Hence for today's visit I intend to

"Does anywhere ever remain pure, unchanged? Sometimes the search for fishing paradise takes you to an industrial estate."

Gone are the past masters and huge carp, but Walker's Devon pond is still a beautiful place

A timeless, fishy looking swim is tested

This powerful, golden carp was anything but "common"!

take a leap backwards and revisit Walker's own favourite approach; no bolt-rigged, bait-dip glugged monstrosity but simply a large, free-lined, piece of bread paste in the margins.

Interestingly, in *Stillwater Angling* Walker admits a dislike for the disturbance of heavy leads, contenting himself with just a single split shot down the line to pin the last few feet of line to the bottom. Onto the hook goes a ball of bread paste about the size of a walnut. The old carp pioneers would have buried the hook inside this. Mine will be hair rigged. It seems curious to think that bread, once the staple of carp fishing, is now something of an "alternative" bait for a generation of anglers who swear by boilies and pellets.

Two luxuries I won't deprive myself once it gets dark, are bite alarms and bait runner reels. Walker himself designed perhaps the first ever prototype alarm—not to sit behind all day but specifically for night fishing when takes were hard to detect. As for reels, the pioneers had no such thing as "free spool" models and would either have coils of loose line ready for a running fish, or simply keep a loose drag before tightening up during the fight.

Having arrived at this classic carp pool in a hastily executed escape plan after work, it's a relief to settle down in a quiet corner. With a plop the first bait lands in the margin, another aimed further out towards a bushy, deeper area. A scattering of bread mash and hempseed finish the job and I'm just about ready to rest my legs and brew a mug of tea.

SLOWLY, THE HISS OF PASSING CARS SUBSIDES. The metal dinosaurs on the quarry fall silent and all is calm. By night

Walker's *Stillwater Angling* is still an inspiring read

the pond is strangely restored to former glory. Bats flicker across the pool; the moon swims beside the lilies. I lay back and relax but the anticipation lingers, heightened by the occasional splash in the gloom.

As one o'clock approaches I'm starting to ponder whether these clay pit carp exist only in the faded pages of a bygone era, when the line gives a quick judder. Moments later the alarm sounds as the line tightens and I lift into something solid. For around ten seconds of exhilaration I'm

scrabbling somewhere between panic and control before the hook pulls out. I add my swearwords to those of past anglers and decide to sleep on it.

I'm snoozing between wake and sleep as the light returns to the lake, along with suspicious trails of fine bubbles. The moorhens are squabbling, but that is about the only drama. And so, feeling restless, I declare a temporary truce with the carp and break out the float tackle to see if I can catch a tench, or anything to lift my spirits.

When I reach some of the leafier swims that could have been lifted directly out of a classic illustrated fishing guide, I quickly begin catching small bream on paste before the inevitable happens. The float walks and dips unwaveringly before the lilies rock in the wake of something much stronger. Either it's the world's strongest tench or, dare I believe, one of a long line of carp that have tormented and thrilled so many visitors before me.

The sheer power is hair-raising on an Avon rod. The whole thing sweeps round as, twice, the fish plunges for the edge and almost finds sanctuary. Inch by inch I guide it towards the bank, slightly shaky with a cocktail of sleep deprivation and raw nerves. For perhaps five minutes neither side wins, but eventually the fish tires and the net is sunk. It is a common carp of no more than 10 to 12lb, cream-bellied, bright gold and brilliantly proportioned. 50 years ago this was a specimen fish; today it is a creature that wouldn't merit a second glance from any diehard specimen hunter. Nevertheless, I'm knocked out by its raw strength and exceptional beauty.

The machines on the quarry grumble to life as I tear myself away, work-bound. With the morning rush building on the main road, the magic of the place seems to ebb away a little. Nonetheless, the fact that Abrook Pond exists at all is reason to be thankful and, who knows, perhaps future generations will also add their own stories to the pool? ●

The Madness of King Zyg

SITTING BENEATH THE JUTTING HEAD OF A SWORDFISH, you quickly realise the bar at Anglers Paradise is not your average watering hole. A giant eel hovers behind glass. Rods, reels and strange lures join beer mats and bottles. But then you wouldn't expect anything less of its owner Zyg Gregorek: big game fanatic, innovative fishery owner, brewer of lethal wines, tackle obsessive and lovable lunatic. It's difficult to know where to start and which Zyg we might meet today.

Zyg hit the headlines last week in a narrow escape from Karachi, one of the world's most exciting but dangerous angling locations. It's something of a mercy that he's sitting here today, able to share a tipple with us at all. Typically, at an age where most men revert to gardening and comfortable footwear, his passion for adventure fishing remains undiminished. If anything though, Zyg talks down the element of risk and wouldn't rule out a return—although he adds: "I wouldn't take my wife." The Lifetime Achievement award he went to collect from local dignitaries had a close scrape too—the glass trophy itself being stowed away whilst bullets ricocheted around the workshop where it was made. A destination to cross off the holiday list, Karachi police aren't always much friendlier than the locals, having misidentified rod tubes as weapons on previous trips. A far cry from sleepy Devon, that's for sure.

You get the feeling Zyg is used to unusual twists and scrapes with danger however, as he reveals from early childhood experience. "My first fishing was at age five or six in Tanzania, by the sea. I noticed fish sheltering in old pieces of pipe and would jam my hands over the ends to trap them. I also used to chase mud skippers—until one time I got caught fast in quicksand and was lucky to be pulled out alive." He admits he was fearlessly naive as a child: "I also got chased by a hippo after throwing a coconut at it." Other madness included a brush with a lion and near abduction by a passing tribesman.

Despite the tropical backdrop of a childhood spent in various different countries however, Gregorek's family were refugees. "My family suffered real deprivation," he recalls. "We were once rich, but under the communist regime in Poland we lost everything." Fleeing from the horrors of a murderous dictatorship, the boy was forced to grow up fast. "I was used to hearing 'no' when I asked for things," he explains, "but in a way it set me up because I've always had to struggle and try my hardest. Looking back this makes it even more satisfying to achieve what I have."

Wine brewer, big game angler and lovable lunatic Mr Zyg Gregorek

When Zyg came to England at the age of seven, life didn't get any easier or less eventful as he moved from school to school. "Believe it or not in my early years I was very shy," he remembers. "I spoke very little English at first and as a newcomer I often got picked on. But this made me very resilient."

It was the making of him and young Zyg quickly learned to be resourceful. "I used to breed rabbits and budgerigars to sell, partly because I never got any pocket money," he explains. The beginnings of a future fishery boss were already being sown it seems, while he also learned other skills from his family. "Grandad used to distil his own drinks and so in time I learned this too." It's a skill he still uses to this day to produce his legendary, potent home-brewed wine.

ZYG PASSED FROM SCHOOL THROUGH TO UNIVERSITY VIA A HUNDRED ENTERPRISES from building sites to all manner of odd-jobs. "I had to do all sorts of things to enjoy what others had—and that meant a knack for doing the unusual" he says. Conventional he may never have been, but Zyg always found a way. In between daily pressures he also discovered roach, chub and trout on the Thames.

His graft and knack for business saw him hit success in the insurance business after university. He flourished in London but admits: "I reached the stage where I was making money but began to hate it."

A change of scene to fish farming was "a gamble", he confesses. "I sold everything and moved." His pioneering efforts in

The bar at Angler's Paradise is a world of piscatorial oddities.

"At an age where most men revert to gardening and comfortable footwear, his passion for adventure fishing remains undiminished."

breeding ornamental fish such as golden tench were a period he describes as "my most successful failure—it didn't quite work but I learned a hell of a lot".

Anglers Paradise began in 1985 with just one lake and five villas, a far cry from today's complex. But the project steadily grew, not only with its creator's eccentric mix of species but also a new vision. "When we began the coarse angler was second best," says Zyg. "Garden shed accommodation was normal. We set new standards of quality."

Today the complex is another world: some 30 lakes over 250 acres and a list of guests which reads like a *Who's Who* of angling stars. But it is the many other visitors who make the place what it is. "I have guests from 1985 that still return and visitors from all over the world," Zyg says proudly. "Those who came as children are now bringing their own kids. It's something special."

Is he still ambitious? "Yes, and why not? I've only just started as far as I'm concerned," he laughs. "We've always reaped profits into improving the complex—even in the recession."

The desire to succeed also applies to his passion for big game fishing, from international trophies to a string of world records. Amidst a hectic working life Zyg still finds time for the odd "research" trip and has more wild, fishy tales than a great white has teeth; stories of giant marlin,

Eels, catfish and even a shoal of golden rudd complete a collection of cased weirdness

billfish and ravenous sharks—nd you guessed it, more scrapes with danger. Such as the trip Down Under when he nearly became a salt water croc's breakfast. The guide had already spotted the tonne or so of croc before near disaster: "The boat had drifted, hit the mangroves and I fell," Zyg recalls. "I had a gash in my side and was covered in mud and slime. Somehow or other I managed to get back in the boat." Sane mortals would find a hospital—not Zyg. "Within an hour I had my first barramundi," he grins. "The next day I realised just how badly injured I was. I don't quite know how I survived the flight home."

Amongst other achievements however, Zyg is also hugely proud of his capture of the complex's first 30lb carp—tamed on a split cane rod and float set up and played with a stinking hangover to boot!

Another glass of Zyg's wine and I might tip over. It tends to give a man ideas. Unhinged ones. In my own madder moments when I imagine a future Britain as some kind of angling Utopia, I picture Zyg as its president. The economy would be based entirely on fishing tackle. The currency wouldn't be pounds or euros but flies. Fishing would be free and participation compulsory. State meetings would be attended in waders. All roads would be replaced by canals. Because of a fish-heavy diet we would all live to the age of 107 and be geniuses.

Along with more bottles of distilled madness, the many mementos in the bar tell their own thousand tales—but if you want more you'll have to go and share a jar with the man himself. And the adventure isn't over yet. In front of the titanic dentistry of a shark's jaws I ponder if Zyg is as crazy as ever. "I hope so," he says. And so do we—fishing would be a duller place without him. ●

Chilling with Char

EXACTLY HOW FAR ANGLERS WILL GO TO CATCH A STUPID, COLD-BLOODED FISH IS SOMETHING THAT MUST BAFFLE ORDINARY HUMAN BEINGS. We will wait all day and stay out all night. We will get up at stupid o'clock and still be late home. But in the field of sheer bloody-

minded insanity, the anglers of Norway must top the list. Take biting winds, subzero temperatures and lakes that resemble snow fields and there are still fish to be caught.

Or so I'm hoping at Alta Airport, as large flakes settle outside and I wonder just how it is possible that it is already spring in England. Stepping out into the snow, my friend Geir Sivertzen grins as we get into his car and head north. The road from Alta is an ice-hardened corridor to the wilderness where we'll be fishing for Arctic char, the beautiful fire-bellied fish of Norway's mountain lakes. Aside from the white spray of a single passing truck, the atmosphere is one of stark isolation. But luckily for us, the snow is not thick enough to slow a swift passage towards the high grounds.

Our destination of Skaidi, meaning "meeting of rivers", sounds tempting until you look in vain for waterways totally buried in the snow. Picturing a grand, desolate building like something out of *The Shining*, I'm relieved to find Hotel Skaidi a cosy place, promising a night of warmth before we set up camp in the mountains.

Over a coffee, Norwegian experts Morten Stensaker and Geir Sivertzen provide a crash course on the strange tackle required for ice fishing. Next to a colossal corkscrew-bladed drill sits the shortest, cutest fishing rod you've ever seen. By jigging a flashing spoon, we'll aim to draw the fish to a hook baited with maggots.

By morning, even these sons of the north are wondering about the potentially treacherous, Arctic conditions. For perhaps two hours, we huddle in the entrance of the hotel as wind speeds and forecasts are studied. Over my third coffee I try to make out a horizon that seems to have been Tipp-Exed out of existence.

With a break in the wind however, our chance must be taken. Last checks are made with our guide, Jan Johansen, as we pack food, sleeping bags and camping equipment onto snowmobiles. In a buzz of engines, we are tracking our way to the mountains.

The speed of the vehicles and feel of the ice is a little daunting at first, but slowly becomes addictive. Skaidi becomes a mere speck behind us. Trees shoot past and the snow continues to fall.

OUR FIRST STOP IN THE HEIGHTS MUST BE ABOUT THE LEAST OBVIOUS FISHING SPOT I'VE EVER COME ACROSS. In fact, until Jan tells us to stop I haven't a clue that we're in the middle of a frozen lake. The process of preparing a fishing pitch makes strange, enthralling viewing to an Englishman: after digging away the surface snow with a shovel, a giant hand drill is cranked through a full metre of ice. Once the tip plunges through, cold water floods upwards and you have a perfect little fishing hole. A reindeer skin then keeps your backside from freezing.

My first assumption that the fish will be at vast depths proves false, as our rigs find less than six feet of water. Char are sometimes taken in even less, and Morten tells me it is

A giant corkscrew drill creates the perfect fishing hole

a particular thrill to peer into the hole and watch them approach a baited lure.

With a jigging action on the rod tips, we work our spoons to life. A special insert sends out flashes of electric light to set up some kind of bizarre, Arctic char disco. Attached just eight inches below, the bait wavers enticingly. It's weird enough to be sitting on a giant ice sheet above shoals of fish, but within 10 minutes comes a frantic, twitching bite. Disbelieving, I crank up my first char through the glassy hole. The fish is totally unworldly. Dotted olive sides give way to an insanely bright orange belly. Lying in barren white snow the fish seems little short of a miracle.

With the snow and ice literally whitening my beard, I'm quite glad when a move is suggested. Still higher in the mountains we travel, in search of another secret lake known for specimen char.

Knowing where to start on this great snow plain seems like perfect madness as we take turns drilling. Over the course of a few hours, we produce more holes than you'd find in a packet of Polos. The only process I can liken it to is a giant game of battleships; for every miss, another hole produces a tremble on the rod tip. The fish form definite clusters and the action can be sudden and hectic. Playing these aggressive fish on a toy of a rod is a childish delight.

More importantly, our catch will form tonight's fry up. With the snowfall building, it's action stations to pitch our tent, and Jan's Norwegian army model has its own stove and chimney. An Eskimo-style wall of snow bricks offers a suitable wind break to one side.

WITH THE ELEMENTS HOWLING OUTSIDE, IT'S SURPRISINGLY WARM UNDER COVER. Fried in butter, the char are utterly delicious. My own rather limited assistance is quickly forgiven as I produce a bottle of whiskey.

Even more civilised is the fact that we're able to continue fishing under wraps. At each corner of the tent is an ice hole and this is perhaps the closest I've ever come to indoor

Fire in the belly:
Arctic char are stunning creatures

angling. Warmed by the stove, we add a few more char before bedtime, while the eerie glow of the Northern Lights outside only increase the feeling that I'm already asleep and this is all a strange dream.

More lakes are discovered the next day as we explore the heights, racing up slopes to continue drilling and fishing at over 1,000 feet above sea level. I also discover more about the char of these waters and the guide's tricks. Both parties could be described as Arctic specialists, well-accustomed to long winters. No other freshwater fish ventures as far north as the char. And in total contrast to the UK, they're so prolific here that Jan believes that regularly removing some for the frying pan is the way to increase the average size.

It's odd to think that over the summer this Arctic paradise transforms into a sunny land of pure lakes and rocky trails. As we exit the heights, torrents of snow render land and sky into one continuous blur of white. Despite the cold, I'm sorry to leave. I keep hoping for one last rattle on the rod tip, but as the weather worsens it never arrives.

When even the Norwegians are looking at the sky and muttering ill words, you know it isn't time to hang around. With the gear bundled onto the snowmobiles, we spit and roar back down the slopes, looking for civilisation, or some semblance of it. But for now there is no sun and no horizon, no difference between land and sky, only white. ●

The author wishes to thank Skaidi Hotel (www.skaidihotel.no) and www.visitnorthernnorway.com

The Scales of Madness

WE HAD JUST LANDED A BIG FISH AND THE WORDS TOOK ME BY SURPRISE. "I haven't bothered carrying scales for a while now." We had a deep-bodied perch in the net and were in that elated rush that follows the kind of monster you don't see too often. But my companion didn't share the same clamouring to know its weight. "Isn't catching it enough?" he asked.

The idealist in me would certainly agree. Take a step back and you sometimes have to ask yourself, why do we need to reduce every decent fish we catch to a cold statistic? Because that is all it is, a number. Something for fishing anoraks to log in a notebook or, worse, to stick under peoples noses in tackle shops or the dreaded pages of Facebook.

Since when did fishing become so fixated with size? For my father's generation, the tackle and many techniques were so crap that any above average fish seemed to be greeted with jubilation. But some clever Dick, Walker to be precise, opened a whole Pandora's box of worms by introducing a systematic way of targeting the biggest fish, to the exclusion of the rest. Decades later, we have a world of electronic alarms, artificially stocked lakes, serial rods and serial bores.

Perhaps I just don't get "specimen hunting". The very term sounds faintly ridiculous, while the process itself can be painfully attritional. To fish with focus, often for just one species with a particular target weight in sight, can be a soul-destroying task. In some cases, when weeks can pass without success, it becomes closer to masochism than fishing. And while I admire the catches, I don't envy the countless days of tinned food, cold monotony and haemorrhoids.

Do I like catching large fish? Certainly. Who doesn't? Sometimes I specifically target them; occasionally I even catch one or two. But do they define the entire reason I go fishing? No, not on your life. For me the real giants are an occasional bonus, best summed up by US writer John Geirach as "that once or twice a season 'oh shit!' fish".

AS LITTLE AS IT INFLATES MY EGO, I FIND TROTTING FOR AVERAGE ROACH MORE RIVETING THAN SITTING IT OUT FOR LARGE CARP. I would rather fly fish a small river for modest chub than sit behind buzzers for a six-pounder. That's just the way I'm wired. If I enjoy it and it's interesting I don't give a hoot if the fish aren't huge. My only concern is that in the midst of our mania for big fish, the innocence and simple pleasure of fishing are trampled on.

Another angling friend once kept company with a deadly serious big fish man. On their way to a noted specimen water, they were distracted by a small river along the way. The whole place looked beautiful: clear, stony water and visible, if

"In the midst of our mania for big fish, the innocence and simple pleasure of fishing are being trampled on."

In an anonymous survey 83% of anglers exaggerated their catches. The rest were just outright liars

modest-sized, chub and barbel. My friend was spellbound. Mr Big Fish took one look and said: "I'm not going to win the f***ing Drennan Cup fishing there."

But am I any more of a purist? I'm currently looking at my scales and feeling a bit like a hypocrite. I bought a posh set which I'm sad enough to test every season to check the accuracy. Could I fish for a whole year like my friend, without them, I wonder? I'm not so sure. Perhaps I should try it. Pounds and ounces would be replaced by terms such as "quite big", "not so big", or "bloody huge". I would find myself using the time-honoured fisherman's method of stretching out my hands in the direction of disbelieving mates.

The trouble is, people would still want to know. They would ask the weight. "Quite big", or "bigger than the one I had last season", isn't enough. Perhaps I too would still be seized by the desire to know, to slap a statistic on the catch as if the experience itself were not enough. People might think my lack of scales meant I wasn't a "serious" angler or, heaven forbid, I was someone who just went fishing because they enjoyed it.

But why do we always need to know? Why is that number so important? Perhaps it is because even in a sport as meditative as fishing, we feel the need to keep score. It is virtually impossible to accurately measure the skill or ability it took to catch any given fish, let alone the sense of satisfaction. The weight is the one concrete part we can record.

Herein lies the rub. Not only do these statistics turn friends into bitching rivals and honest men into liars, they're not always a reliable guide to anything. What angling figures describe most clearly is a spectacularly uneven playing field. I've often thought that specimen awards should be measured in comparison to venue records rather than

At a little less than twenty pounds, I was absolutely gutted to catch this carp, as you can probably tell

national standards. Is a fit 10lb carp from a wild pond the same as a fat old mirror bombarded with free bait? Is a wily old 15lb pike from a small river a lesser capture than a fish that has grown to double that size on a diet of artificially stocked rainbow trout? And why is there never an award for "most beautiful fish"?

WHERE THE FINAL WEIGHT IS THE ONLY IMPORTANT STATISTIC, THE END JUSTIFIES THE MEANS. I would argue that our methods have, if anything, become cruder and increasingly impersonal the more our fishing gears towards big fish at all costs (bolt-rigging for crucian carp anyone?). It is not enough for a technique to be chosen because it's enjoyable.

What I don't doubt is that there are anglers who get their main kick out of pursuing the biggest fish all the time. And yes, Richard Walker was one of them and remains one of my heroes. But even 60 years ago, he bemoaned the shameless "one-upmanship" that was already creeping into angling. He also believed that any fish that required a landing net was worth catching. How different today's message: catch bigger. Avoid "nuisance fish". Up your PB. Avoid waters that don't contain huge fish.

So will those scales stay in my fishing bag? I'm afraid so. Because someone spotted a huge perch on the canal last week. A 30lb carp might just pick up my sweetcorn on the gravel pit. But a bit of perspective never goes amiss either.

Happiness is not a figure. It is found in the present moment, not past glories or future targets. The only fish that truly matters is the next one that bites, while the best catch you will ever make is the feeling of simple contentment just to be there, fishing. ●

Small Dreams on a Millstream

I MUST HAVE DRIVEN PAST THE TINY RIVER EXE TRIBUTARY A HUNDRED TIMES BEFORE ACTUALLY STOPPING FOR A CLOSER LOOK. For over a decade, I have simply ignored this tiny blue line on the map in favour of bigger waters. Because for any romantic notions I might hold, I'm also lulled by the promise of bigger fish and the siren song of countless fishing articles that tell us to "catch bigger!". Such is the soul of modern angling; like diners at a fast food outlet, we are constantly urged to go super-sized, as if what we have is never enough. But what pretty, smaller waters we miss in the process.

Unless you were to delve behind Exeter's posher suburbs, you might never realise this mile or so of water even existed. It's no major river. It's fairly bloody tiny if I'm honest. And yet so beautiful you could stick it in an art

gallery. Feeding into the grander, muddier main river, the millstream cuts a quiet, stony course among footpaths, leafy tracks and the shell of an old mill. The crematorium sits on one side, the country club on the other. And there in the middle, sandwiched between the golf course and the dead, sits a damned-near-perfect seam of water.

The stream is as shallow as a boyband and full of fish. It's also a place that takes you back to a time when fishing was no more complicated than a stick float and a pint of maggots. Small it may be, but you might find just about anything here. Roach and chub shoal in inches of water, along with scattered gangs of perch and even the odd wandering mullet. Later in the season it's not unusual to find the battered form of a spawned out salmon loitering in one of the pools.

Listening to the tales of some of the old random types on the bank you might think black magic was afoot—tales emerge of floodwater pike and even sea trout. But I tend to fish simply, with the fly rod or trotting with a centrepin.

THIS MORNING, I FIND MYSELF SITTING ON A TINY BRIDGE WHERE THE STREAMBED DROPS INTO A BROADER POOL. Handfuls of maggots are tossed into the current, followed by the float, before rapid dace bites arrive. You might seldom hook anything that requires a net, but each of these little fish is as sparkling and fresh as the next.

You could happily plant yourself in the sun for hours here, but wanderlust usually catches me and I want to see more of the river. Some days I don't feel like I can quit before I've stared into every last corner.

The bushy, overgrown waters are especially inviting. Those bits the odd float or spinner dangles from the branches from a misplaced cast. There are chub here, nosing through sunken roots and undercut banks, often in mere inches of water. They're not exactly world record-sized, but it's curious just how grand a 2lb chub looks when you've been flirting with dace one tenth that size.

Somehow it's all relative, and through the secretive branches of the mill stream lies the quiet truth of fishing: it doesn't really matter how big the fish are. The moment is

One from the rough: a millstream chub

all that matters, when you're peering into the flow of the river and nothing else really exists. And yes, even the smallest water holds magic. It's only our own lack of ability to find the beauty in the little things of life which speaks otherwise.

ALMOST BY DEFINITION, THE FISH THAT LIE IN THE MOST TANGLED, HORRENDOUSLY INACCESSIBLE PLACES BECOME EVEN MORE TEMPTING. The chub in the little pocket before me idle about freely, as if they know perfectly well how nearly untouchable they are. Even the smallest float or feeder would spook these fish and there's hardly room to stand up, let alone make an overhead cast. The answer is to think simpler and shorter. A small fly rod is perfect to flick a little beetle or imitation grasshopper in the path of the fish.

I watch two more chub pass obliviously before taking aim. But if the idea looked simple in your head, the trees have other ideas. The first two casts don't even reach the water, but just the branches. I freeze for a few seconds wondering if I've already spooked the fish, hoping that my bad language hasn't offended the chub.

The next cast is the one I was hoping for, the shot that falls exactly as you meant it and makes you wonder why you ever found it so bloody difficult in the first place. The black, bushy fly settles on the surface and one of the chub makes a bold, instant turn towards it. In a gape of white lips it is gone. I lift without even thinking, the rod bucks and the fish bolts for cover.

You can watch the whole scene unfold on a clear little stream. The effect on the shoal is like a police car meeting a group of hoodlums, chub scattering in all directions and leaving their mate stranded.

The hooked fish is no giant, but with a toothpick of a trout rod in a tight swim, the fight is not without a little drama. In

true chub style, he's mostly splash and no great staying power. He makes a bid for the branches right under my feet but the net is already there. I admire him for just a passing few seconds, before the fish is gone, as if neither of us were ever there.

I head for home later than planned, as usual. Each little bend holds more fish as the spots get more and more impossible. I watch perch hover below a wooden bridge and a wagtail bob on the gravel. I lose a couple of flies and I lose track of time. By the old mill works the dace are rising, but instead of another last cast I just watch them and ponder for a while. All the madness and the miles I travel. All the hours I wait for a few bigger fish. And yet perhaps what I was really looking for all along was just a perfectly laid-back afternoon on a pretty stream. ●

A stealthy, silver dace

YOU'VE NO DOUBT ALREADY HEARD PLENTY ABOUT THEM, OUR POLISH FRIENDS. Hard workers with an unfortunate liking for table-sized carp, if you believe the headlines. You probably meet them every day doing a hundred and one different jobs, not to mention those down on your local water with a fishing rod.

Does their reputation precede them I sometimes wonder? Like the Brits, the Polish love their fishing. But how great are the differences in reality? And how exactly do you reconcile one culture where carp are protected by law and another where they are eaten for Christmas dinner?

I've probably seen the best and the worst to be fair. On the one hand I've met those poachers with limited English, fishing for the pot. Then again, I count Polish catch and release angler and bailiff Seb Nowosiad as one of my most trusted friends. I also owe

Taking cover on the River Odra

Poland greatly for one of its rather unique exports: my girlfriend Paulina. And it was her grand idea for me to cast aside any fixed ideas and travel to Poland to experience a different fishing culture for myself.

IN POLAND'S SOUTH IS THE SO CALLED CITY OF A HUNDRED BRIDGES, Wroclaw, home to the mighty Odra: the country's second biggest river. The self-styled "Venice of the North" has more river views than you can shake a rod at, along with an unusual mixture of old world architecture and modern tower blocks. But as Paulina points out the local sights, my eyes keep being drawn back to the waters.

There are huge bridges and wide, gaping flows here, as well as empty sections being renovated like a strange urban experiment. Fishing is popular here and it's not long before I find two young local anglers, Mateusz and Tomasz (Matt and Tom, if you like) making their way to the river on the bus. Would we like to join them for a crack at some bream? Is the Pope a Catholic?

Some illusions about Polish anglers are quickly dispelled as we tackle up. Both of the lads speak good English, as is typical among young Poles. Nor are these crude anglers: quiver tip rods and fine feeder rigs are assembled.

They fish for pleasure mainly. The occasional fish might be taken home, but this is about sport rather than food and they are well-versed in catch and release fishing. Nor is Poland some kind of free-for-all. If you do decide to take, catches must be recorded, with strict limits on how many an individual may remove. I'm equally surprised to learn that as a new angler Tomasz had to take a test to get his license.

It's a pleasant afternoon on the Odra. The bream won't cooperate, but it's a good chance to practise my slightly dodgy Polish and share some typical fishing fare from these parts: a cold brew with a handful of sunflower seeds. Sport can be excellent here in the right conditions, I'm assured. The bream run to double figures, while roach, perch, carp and all the other usual suspects are present along with the "Amur", a creature somewhere between a grass carp and a mullet, that can grow to a metre long.

The new generation of anglers, like Mat and Tom, are increasingly adopting catch and release

I'm especially interested to ask about lure fishing too, an area where the Polish have a real expertise. The waters of the Odra hold formidable predators: pike, zander and even catfish have fallen to lures for Mateusz. No such excitement today though, so we bid farewell along with the words "Polamania Kija" for good luck—which in Polish literally means "break a rod".

OUR NEXT TRIP TO THE RIVER BANK OCCURS A FEW DAYS LATER as we join Paulina's neighbour and his brother, old school anglers who fish for the table as well as relaxation. I'm not massively keen on the idea of knocking fish on the head, but this is their country not mine.

The older heads are totally different to the younger Poles. They often speak little English and are less open to modern ideas on fish conservation. Fishing is a hobby that ends with a frying pan. But there are deeper reasons too: living through the hardships of communism, the older generation relied on rivers for food.

We couldn't have picked a worse day for rain. Gazing at a fantastically industrial-looking stretch of river under heavy clouds, I joke in broken Polish about the weather being just like in England. Nobody laughs.

Heavy feeders are lobbed out and my other half acts as interpreter as they explain a few mysteries of the Odra. Floating debris and litter add little to the romance of the rising water. The river can flood as horrendously as in Britain, as it did a few years ago here to drown homes and even the local highway.

Conditions are foul, but the locals have a saying here, along the lines of "when it rains like hell, the bream bite well". And it rings true as one of the tips rattles away and a bulky bream is hoisted onto the bank. I know what awaits the fish they cram into a pathetically small keepnet. It seems crude to me, but it won't go to waste. Catches like this will be shared with neighbours and friends.

With the rain falling ever harder, lightning threatens and with only a couple

Are you seriously going to eat that?

of silver bream to add, an early exit looks imminent. To my horror, the large bream is simply tossed into an empty bucket where it flaps, helplessly still alive.

After a 20-minute car journey, I politely thank our hosts for taking us fishing. In return, they dump our unfortunate 5lb bream on the lawn as a gift. I think they are explaining how tasty bream are, while I nod unconvincingly. Even more strangely, I see the bream's tail kick. When it happens a second time, I get a daft idea and take it to a small pond in the family garden.

For a while the fish looks defeated as I hold it upright. A couple of minutes later and I'm about to give up entirely when, to my astonishment, the bream rights itself and swims to the bottom of the pond.

The next morning, I fully expect the bream (now christened "Brian") to be dead. But this is one tough fish. A plan is quickly hatched. We check the neighbours aren't watching and grab a large bucket, before fish and all are hoisted onto the handlebars of a bicycle. The ride to the river is distinctly wobbly as I try to remember to keep on the right side of the road, the bream's tail slapping the side of the bucket.

And so bream and river are reunited. The dark shape of the fish passing into the depths is nothing short of a small miracle. Bizarrely, just we're making our way off, I'm stopped by a local landowner asking my business by the river. It strikes me that I could become the first man ever in Poland to be prosecuted for releasing a fish, instead of taking one for the pot. We communicate in broken German, and he asks no further questions.

Am I about to set a new trend in long distance catch and release here in Poland? I'm not sure whether the bream's original captor would be offended or just baffled

Our rescue plan involved a bicycle and a bucket

by this act. Inevitably, he calls round next evening and asks how the fish was. "Very tasty, thanks!" we nod.

AS WELL AS POLAND'S CITIES AND SUBURBS, IT IS A COUNTRY OF QUIETER SURROUNDINGS AND SOME TRULY BEAUTIFUL WATERS. It's in the mountains of the south in the small town of Sokolowsko that we find a very different taste of Polish fishing.

Once a place bustling with health spas and sanatoriums, this old town now has a sense of scenic isolation. Paint flakes off farm buildings and there is a haunted stillness about the rows of elegant, deserted houses. My better half Paulina once caught trout with her bare hands in the mountain stream here, but since those days poachers have taken virtually every fish in sight.

Up at the foot of the mountains are small, idyllic ponds. The Poles stock these with roach, perch, tench and carp, just like local fishing clubs do in Britain. The first of several we find lies at the foot of a semi-derelict Russian style church. Reeds are swaying slightly in the breeze, lilies dot the water. Around the margins are scrums of clumsy, mating toads. The air is clear, almost alpine, and you couldn't imagine a better spot for a sunny afternoon off.

Sitting on one corner is Marek, an old Pole with a pole. He swings out a slightly clumsy float rig which he rather adeptly uses to catch roach on tiny pieces of bread. For him fishing is about killing a couple of hours after work. He's a gentle soul, and talkative once Paulina gets him on the subject of fishing. The roach he catches are just a bit of sport and will all go back, although he will occasionally keep perch or pike. Interestingly, I also learn that a few catch and release specimen carp fisheries, not so different from our own, are now springing up in Poland. Perhaps the sport vs food debate isn't so clearcut here

A little piece of heaven, near the Czech border

after all? In any case, it seems too perfect an afternoon to talk piscatorial politics with our friend Marek, so we bid him good luck and make our way.

It's a little world apart up here, but I can't help seeing Marek as very similar to many British pleasure anglers. Are we so very different? Conservation still has catching up to do in Poland; older generation Poles do sometimes see ecosystems as just a source of food. But we can't tar them all with the same brush. These are not, by and large, ruthless poachers.

With around a million Poles now in Britain, we had better get used to them. Old school labourers with little English can be a problem. But the better news is that the younger Poles speak English, travel well and embrace new ideas. Poland itself is a great country with its own rich fishing history and who knows, perhaps in time both cultures can learn from each other? ●

Ghost town: buildings stand eerily vacant in the mountain town of Sokolowsko

A cast too far

IS A FISH EVER WORTH TAKING A RISK FOR? In cold, black and white print the answer is a definite no. For the sake of your dignity, let alone your neck, there is a line that must not be crossed. You don't hang around as the spring tide rushes in, or piss about on a gun owner's private land. Nor do you, contrary to the lunacy of some of my less sober mates, go fishing for shark on an inflatable boat.

There's a reason you back away from that treacherous slope or avoid casting into that

particular swim. But just like fish, anglers can be tempted into taking risks. They have hungry eyes and short memories. Let's be honest, who hasn't miraculously not noticed the "No Fishing" signs, or been drunk in charge of a boat on occasion?

Most of us have taken a soaking, lost our favourite lure or climbed over a barbed wire fence.

Experience should be the best teacher. But the fact that fishing kills more participants than virtually any other sport shows we are still suckers for a gamble. Show me that near perfect yet flawed spot, the one where the fish are fat and the odds are slim and I will still probably make the cast.

Of all people, I should know where the line is. At the age of four, I slipped into the River Thames when fishing with my dad. I was soaking and still white with shock after he'd jumped in and lifted me to safety. I may never have fished again had he told my mother, who only found out about this little stunt some 30 years later.

These days I'm not a reckless sort as a rule, but there are still occasional moments. The last instance started with the sight of a big trout. This time it was no accident or sudden lapse of judgment, but a slow turning over a matter of weeks and months.

I'd been fishing most of the summer in and amongst it on a part-pretty, part-flaky trout stream, meandering through a seaside town. Never shy of wading in or ducking branches if required, I had explored most of the water. However, one section of river had always been beyond me. For a good 200 yards the entire flow is contained in a great channel of stone and concrete. The walls each side must be 12 feet high. In places, it resembles a smaller version of the huge stone gutter where the car chase takes place in Terminator 2, had the movie been filmed in a shit seaside town. Even if you could get down there you wonder how the hell you would ever get out.

Towards the end of this section is a lovely, stony crease of water, where the

large trout was almost always sitting. Only when the river was in flood would you find him missing.

I would be lying if I said it was a huge fish. But when most of the natives are eight or so inches, a fish of double that length takes on a dramatic significance. Do fish become more desirable or even appear bigger when they are beyond our reach? This must be how many local myths begin.

But that fish was special. I must have passed the exact spot some 30 times and been hypnotised. Sometimes I'd stand there for many minutes, just watching what it did. I watched it rise for hatching olives and I saw it edge in and out of the flow. The smaller fish stayed well out of its way. Sometimes it would hang there brazenly in full view of onlookers, as if it knew it was untouchable. That fish tortured me.

LOWER IN THE TOWN, DOWN NEAR THE SEA, THE IMPOSSIBLE WALLED SECTION ENDS WITH A SMALL WEIR. Logs choke the bottom and not a lot stirs. The gulls are circling and a loud-mouthed woman is calling out to her dog as if it were an actual person, in between talking shite on her phone. All that separates me from the promised land is a narrow ledge, running alongside the weir.

I have looked at this spot several times in all honesty, never having the guts to proceed. But from now on my visits will be limited, owing to my changing circumstances. My girlfriend is just about to move to the city with me, and while it's great news that she finds me an acceptable human being to live with, it means I will no longer have those glorious couple of hours every Saturday morning before I pick her up from work. It is now or never.

The plan is an uneasy mixture of caution and risk. With only the narrowest of corridors to balance across, I limit myself to just a rod and a few bits in a wading vest. A camera bag could be a total bloody disaster along that wall, although I must take a net to have any chance of landing that beast of a trout.

The first steps are safe, planting my feet and feeling my balance. But ominously, just a matter of inches further, the shelf narrows wickedly. Besides the slope and the threat of the churning water below, that little path to nirvana is less than the width of one my size 14 wading boots. It's at times like this I wish I had a lower centre of gravity and small, nimble feet.

I take a step at a time, shuffling sideways with my back to the wall as things get horribly and progressively more narrow. And then a moment of hesitation. I kid myself that at worst I will get soaked and look like a twat; but I have no idea how deep it is and it looks dreadfully rocky below.

Another three or so steps and I reach a position of no return. I'm locked against the wall, unable to turn around now. So I inch forward, on a tightrope, shitting myself. As the ledge tapers away to nothing, the sill of the weir is just above me, carpeted in weed. It looks slippery, but is the only foothold available and so I draw a deep

Stolen gold, no longer out of reach

breath and plant my right boot on it. I make a little testing movement and, mercifully, it doesn't budge and so I push forward and bring my other foot down. I am safe. Thank goodness, I'm safe.

Wading slowly through the walled section offers that rare feeling of freedom usually reserved for trespassers. Up above the walls is a town of several thousand and yet there is an exquisite type of stolen solitude here. Here I am, hidden from view in a spot that very possibly hasn't been fished in a decade. In spite of the bare concrete walls, plants spring from tiny gaps and the river bed looks stony and rich.

The first trout I see are typical natives, small and pretty but nothing epic. I quickly make a few casts and get them rising to a small dry fly, hoping to get my eye in for bigger things to come. Eager they might be, but several also flee, no matter how carefully I seem to wade. And then it dawns on me—for weeks I've assumed that catching the big trout will be a formality provided I can only get into position. But just one spooked fingerling could crash upstream and wreck the whole plan. My footsteps get slower and for a time, I stop playing with the runts.

WHEN I REACH IT, THE LAIR OF THE BIG ONE LOOKS DIFFERENT FROM STREAM LEVEL. Through the glare, all I can see is yet another eight-inch tearaway. I keep a safe distance and loiter on the spot, wondering if the game is already over. But no, there he is, in the shallow head of the little run. There is no obvious hatch, other than a few

midges and he rises to the surface just once in what feels like a small eternity, taking something I can't even see.

By this time, my patience is out and so I make a cast with a tiny emerger. It's not the best shot, but the fish sidles across the flow for a look. He comes incredibly close, before sliding away again. I pause for a minute or so before making another shot; exactly the same happens, like an action replay. Bugger.

I flirt with the idea of a nymph, but the water looks inches deep and I'm not convinced. So instead I decide to go for broke and pick a big, juicy caddis, reasoning that I'll get a reaction one way or another, whether it's a definite rise or game over.

If anything I cast too close to him, but the fish immediately comes up for a lingering glance at the bigger fly. Almost out of frustration I give a twitch and, just as it looks like he'll leave it, lips gape, the line pulls tight and there is a berserk thrashing at the surface.

The next couple of nerve-shredding minutes are a mess of shifting power and lunges all over the river, during which, if I'm honest, I'm lucky to stay connected. Feeling the fish flail in just about every direction available in the shallow water is an experience somewhere between pleasure and pure tension. With nowhere to go, it even makes a salmon style leap, before coming straight for the near bank, where the fight gets dirty. For a wretched few seconds, the fish tries to spin behind me and find a gap in the wall, as I'm forced to lurch around and hold on.

Eventually, the fight slows and there is no escape. Not for the first time in the day, I feel a massive wave of relief as I finally capture a fish that only just fits in my trout scoop. And what a creature it is, wild-eyed and stamped with black, blue and gold. A stolen treasure perhaps, but one I return to the stream knowing that no one else will find.

The only thing that removes the afterglow is the sobering reality that I do not know how to get back out of the river. The only alternative to the narrow ledge where I came in is another weir upstream. Just by a ford where cars splash through, it is an embarrassing prospect to scramble up one side of the weir. Onlookers keep peering down, semi-amazed to see a human being down in the concrete gutter. So for a while, I keep fishing, getting a few bites but not worrying if I catch anything.

With a quick break in the human traffic, I then wade quickly to the left. Pacy, broken water deepens and the bottom squidges nastily. Silty clouds billow around my waist. Another couple of steps and I get that horrible cool sensation of water lapping up to my chest, but by some lucky miracle I can feel the bottom starting to shallow again. Step by step, I haul myself up, using a combination of wall and weir until I'm knelt at the top, wet, relieved and happily resolved never to pull the same stunt again. Unless I see an even bigger trout. ●

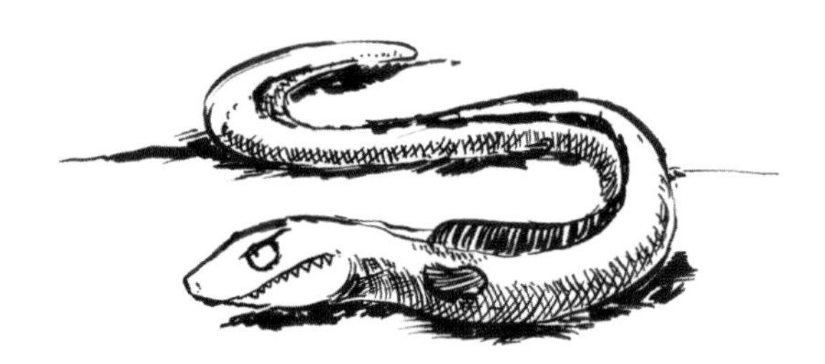

The Strange appeal of the Eel

IS THERE A LESS FASHIONABLE FISH IN ANGLING THAN THE EEL? Let's face it, you either love them or, in the case of the majority, you loathe them. For many, this is barely a fish, but a thing of the night. A swallower of hooks and creator of writhing tangles. Who in their right mind would fish deliberately for eels?

Eel fishermen are a rare breed. For reasons the rest of us miss, these creatures weave their slimy spell on a select few nutters, drawn to their weird mystery. Get beyond the slimy, snake-like form, pause for a moment and the attraction is simple enough: in today's tidy world of predictable, stocked lakes, the eel represents something primal and unpredictable. No maniac ever introduced eels to a fishery and with their long life cycle and uncanny freedom of movement you have a prime recipe for intrigue.

Eels are a species that have a strange habit of wriggling their way back into my consciousness. They also take me back to childhood and evenings on the river; the evening growing dimpsy, a roach pole catapulted over with a grating, writhing presence; the resulting frenzy of eel, line and split shot on the bank.

Eels are also the saviour or the curse of the semi-competent angler, depending on how you look at it. My father and I used to fish the Thames with Fred, the school caretaker. Old silver-haired Fred's line was so thick he only ever seemed to catch eels. Dad was always too polite to say anything, and as Fred turned the air blue I was the only one who seemed to enjoy them.

Years later I rediscovered the writhing pulse of the eel in muddy Somerset. "England's premier eel fishing region," is not exactly the sort of accolade that brings visitors in their droves, but to a tiny few there is promise. The region is awash with dirty rivers, accidental ponds and old clay pits. The eels pour into ditches and drains, the flood water affording freedom of movement for things that slither. Here there are not only odd tales, but strange old ways of catching these slippery customers. Men turn up in dented Land Rovers clutching nets. Money and sometimes blows are exchanged each spring as the young "glass eels" run through the Parrett.

THE STRANGE BUSINESS OF "CLOTTING" FOR EELS IS AN EVEN OLDER ODDITY, which dates back to earlier centuries. It involves a large bunch of worms presented not on hooks but wool. Raymond Perrett's description in the classic *Eels: How to Catch Them* sheds some light: "The eels are attracted by a large bunch of worms which are threaded onto worsted or twine. They hold onto this either from greed or because their teeth get entangled." It sounds bizarre, but his account continues: "A stout pole is used and the line tied securely

"For reasons most of us miss, these creatures weave their slimy spell over a select few nutters, drawn to their weird mystery."

to the end.... Upon getting a bite the bunch of worms is quickly swung out and given a smart shake so that any eel holding on drops off into a waiting tub."

At some point I just had to try it. A "stout pole" was procured for thirty pence at a garden centre before I went to buy some wool at the craft shop, the strongest and reddest available. I dug the worms myself, picking them from the grass and the ooze of the compost heap.

One thing that doesn't change in a century is your typical eel hotspot. I found myself in a suitably grubby swim where a muddy little drain meets an even muddier river and began threading worms onto a generous clump of wool. Dropping this bizarre concoction into the waters below I wondered for a moment what exactly any onlookers would think I was playing at, but then quickly remembered I was in Somerset.

The first response arrived quickly and with conviction. A couple of little plucks at first. A little pause. Then another knock, before the cane pole started bouncing like a thing possessed. I pulled up and sure enough, there was a lively eel attached to the wool. Victory was short lived on snatching the line up however, as a foot or so of wriggling eel

tradition a little better. This was work for real men, with stout arms and grubby hands. An expert "Clotter" (or should that be "clot"?) would have positioned his bucket or barrel as near to the feeding eels as possible, snapping the pole aloft in an instant to drop each writhing critter into the waiting container. The advantage of this is clear—with no hooks to remove our eel man could be fishing again in an instant and the catch would be undamaged and in perfect condition to sell. From my own cack-handed efforts, I can tell you that it was an art form requiring no small measure of dexterity and skill. In the heyday of eel fishing, an old bath tub was one popular method for amassing a collection of eels. Amazingly, this odd practice was still used in the mid 20th century. Just don't expect to see state of the art clotting gear in the glossy tackle catalogues any time soon.

dropped back into the soup below. The same pattern kept repeating: a few taps, a violent hammering on the end of the pole and then an eel in mid air, not keen on letting go of its dinner whilst equally not keen on being yanked into mid air.

The process was hardly pretty, or efficient either, but as I collected a few small eels in the bucket I began to understand the

BUCKETS OF SMALL EELS ARE ONE THING, BUT WHAT OF THOSE REAL GIANTS THAT OCCASIONALLY EMERGE? Countless tales of big eels exist, from outlandish bullshit to far more probable accounts. 50 years ago Perrett wrote that "Much bigger eels than the current rod-caught record do exist. I am sure." Today's eel fanatics echo the same belief. You might well say that the story of eel fishing is one of ignorance as well as

"Eel fishing is sport for the brave… sleep can be impossible, not to mention inadvisable"

knowledge, however. The truth is slippery and elusive as *Anguilla Anguilla* itself; the harder you try to get a firm hold, the more it squirms beyond your grasp. About their life cycle we now know a little more. Unlike our ancestors, who believed that eels could be conjured by throwing black horsehair into running water, we know that the species spawns some 3,000 miles away in the Sargasso. We also know that the eel is slow-growing and long lived: the oldest recorded specimen was 84 years old.That's older than Bruce Forsyth. Possibly. The real giants are those that no longer migrate, thriving in secluded lakes with abundant prey.

Somerset is still arguably the best eel fishing region in the UK, a place of old mires and brick pits which form classic haunts. Picking up the trail on Trinity Waters, Bridgwater, I found several of the National Anguilla Club old boys out fishing on a muggy evening. "Eels are a big unknown," one of the old heads told me, "and that's a very rare thing in fishing nowadays." For strange Somerset lads, it can be a lifetime obsession. "We used to catch the small ones on anything—when we had no pocket money for maggots, bacon rind did the trick."

Today's target is no bootlace however, but a beast as thick as a trucker's wrist. It goes without saying that strong tackle is required here. Thankfully we've come a long way since Perrett's day, when anglers resorted to piano wire to avoid being smashed by the formidable strength of a big eel. But a five-pounder can fight titanically hard and requires stout carp tackle and bite proof leaders at minimum.

However, while the power of a hooked eel can be brutal, the actual bites from the big ones can be more sneaky. These are old, wily fish, cautious of resistance and wary of any angling pressure. Several other stereotypes are also quickly broken as I breach some of the finer points of eel fishing under the incessant tapping of rain on a sodden brolly. While I had these creatures down as scavengers, talk to the eel club boys and a truer picture is of active, adaptable hunters which will happily scythe down the bite-sized rudd and roach which teem in commercial fishing lakes. They are also surprisingly fragile, hence the need for an early strike and care on the bank. Deep hooked eels are unlikely to survive capture.

As the eel boys knuckle down, I bid goodnight and good luck to the youngest of them, teenager Regan Walker (a mere "elver" you might say) who already has the stomach for eel fishing. And I have to admire his pluck, because he seems to be looking forward to the night more than I am.

Under the moonlight and a shelter, eel fishing is sport for the brave. You will receive many taps and pulls from small eels for one thing. Sleep can be almost impossible, not to mention inadvisable if you are fishing anywhere near snags. Regardless, I tend to lie there uneasily when eel fishing; and when it's wet or pitch black I'm not entirely sure if I want that next bite to arrive or not.

At Trinity Waters, I was rewarded with just one moment of excitement. It was just as the evening darkened and my thoughts began to wander to hot food that something made the indicator rise and my heart freeze. I struck to feel a weight, a sudden wrenching, then nothing. The marks on the bait were typical: dislodged scales and two scathing jaw marks. I couldn't tell you whether I was more disappointed or relieved, but this time the eel had slithered beyond grasp. ●

Escape from Dartmoor

THE GUIDEBOOKS PROMISE WIDE OPEN SPACE, STIRRING VIEWS AND GRANITE TORS. But arrive on a typically cool morning in Dartmoor and you might find the whole place lost in heavy, cryptic fog. As we pick a wary course along crooked roads the mist hangs thick as soup. Standing stones hover in the dawn; half-dozing sheep gather like old ladies on their way to church.

Fog and solitude on the rocky River Dart

Cherry Brook: A real schoolboy's stream

For the angler though, Dartmoor has a simple, primal appeal. Its boulder-strewn rivers and savagely beautiful trout take fishing back to its fundamentals: a fly rod, a few basics, miles and miles of stony solitude. The fish are easy to catch but even easier to spook, perfectly adapted to their craggy ancestral home.

The Two Bridges Hotel is one of several oddly refined starting points, where old well-to-do types park Bentleys and kids skip stones. The bridge is a favourite place for onlookers to indulge in a little trout spotting of their own. But the parked cars and artificial flies caught in trees quickly point you towards the open moor beyond.

On the approach to the Dart, stone paths soon give way to ferns and boggy moss. By half past 10 the fog still hasn't lifted, the mist still clinging the harsh beauty and rocky turns of the East Dart. It is this soft veiled menace and close atmosphere that inspired Arthur Conan Doyle to frame *The Hound of the Baskervilles* here on the moor.

Today, thankfully, the only hounds are all fastened to leads. The usually free rising trout are yet to do just that and so exploring with a little nymph is our opening shot and hardly a shooting offence. A tiny, beaded hare's ear is lethal in these shallow waters, suspended just beneath a dry, provided the fish don't spot you first.

The first fish I discover are not with the nymph but the naked eye, fleeing upstream and away from my over-enthusiastic entry. No undue cause to worry though, because trout are everywhere here. A phenomenon in their own right, these Dartmoor brownies are a unique and ancient strain. These are not fat, farm reared trophy trout but have existed for eons, long before the moor was invaded by coachloads of daytrippers in daft hats.

In a world obsessed with sizes, weights and figures the trout of the moors make a perfect exception. "Wild" is an understatement for these dark, wily, predators. In places the stream is littered with them. These are creations of keen eyes, greedy mouths and big heads. When viewed from above some appear virtually black, while in the hand you find a riot of spots, flecks of bronze, copper and gold. A half-pounder here could be a very old fish and one to give a dashing, jolting display on light tackle.

With a stealthier entrance on the next bend encountered, the wet fly is quickly smashed by a leaping, dark gold trout. And another. Picking the fish out of the shallows feels like a primal experience. It's something of a clash to pit the measured elegance of flyfishing against such a backdrop: the jaguar spots of the fish, the blackened stones and pale sand of the river bed, the wild moor; these are the sensations of the Dartmoor angler.

BY SLOW MEASURES THE FOG FINALLY DISSIPATES LEAVING A CRISP, SUNNY MORNING. The West Dart sparkles and the birds come out. By 11, sporadic little olives peel off the water, intercepted by a nearby finch as well as the trout. There is only one, obvious choice to make and it's small and dry.

I could wax lyrical to you about species-specific imitations and special patterns, but frankly it would be bordering on pointless because for most of the time anything small and dark will work.

A small but exquisitely marked moorland brownie

When I first ventured up here I wasn't altogether surprised to learn that some of the local specialists used only two or three fly patterns. The wild look here can be deceptive and the influence of past generations is subtly present in many of these streams, where boulders and rocks have been shifted to form deeper pockets and pools. Such ad hoc habitat improvements were especially valuable in periods such as the Second World War, when families sheltering away from the destruction of German bombing raids on Devon's larger towns were grateful to add fresh trout to their meagre rations.

Today we have no need to remove fish and barbless hooks dominate. Should such a concept exist here, we would reach a bag limit with break neck speed, not that numbers matter up on the moor. It is an exercise in stealth and simplicity. Very few of the trout would earn jealous glances from your friends but each is as a wild treasure. The best of the morning comes, as is often the case, from a deeper bend. Beside a rocky hollow the dry is neatly picked off and for a few glorious seconds the four-weight takes a deeper, kicking curve. Even so, this star prize is still perhaps not quite the length of a school ruler.

A WELL-EARNED LUNCH STOP IS NEXT, BEFORE WE CONTINUE ACROSS THE MOOR AND ROLL DOWN ROAD TO THE VILLAGE OF POSTBRIDGE, a lane said to be haunted by the "hairy hands" of Dartmoor. After a series of freak accidents early in the 20th century, stories rapidly spread about a pair of spectral hands which are said to seize the steering of a car or bike with a vice like grip and force the traveller to crash. One unfortunate case was that of Dr E H Helby, the medical officer for Dartmoor Prison, whose motorcycle and side car slewed off the road in June 1921. He was killed in the crash, although two young daughters of the prison governor riding in the sidecar survived. Call me a sceptic, but I'm inclined to think that poor visibility, along with the

narrowness and wonky camber of the road may have had something to do with the accidents.

Today though, it is no spectral hands that tempt us to swerve off the road but some of the daintiest and downright cutest trout streams you ever set eyes upon. The Cherry Brook is one of the best known and most delightful of all. On first inspection you might wonder if this gurgling brook was capable of holding fish of any description. Often little wider than a rod's length, it possesses a surprising depth and an incredible head of greedy little trout.

Cherry Brook is a stream to approach on your hands and knees with the mindset of a kid. Such are its cramped dimensions and overgrown sides that casting is often all but impossible here. Crane your neck too far over the edge and you will see mad, dark, wild things shooting around the gravel, by which time it's too late. Carefully touch the surface with a fly however, and the results are instant and explosive.

A few hours are more than enough to sample some devilishly good fun on Cherry Brook, where the trout are diminutive but insanely greedy, not to mention brilliantly dashed with colour. Our day ends in a real heatwave, by Dartmoor standards at least, and you might be forgiven for creaking at the knees a little, such is the scrambling, improvised experience of the Dartmoor fly rod.

The obstacle course that forms the moor is also the reason why it made an ideal site for a prison, rendering escape an awkward task for the plucky few who have attempted the feat. Escapees faced not only miles of boggy ground, but dogs and guns. Joseph Denny, a West Indian convict, attempted to set the prison on fire; others made "bone keys" from meal time scraps to pick locks. Others stole horses to aid their escape, while more recent times saw one of the least exciting car chases in criminal history when a desperate inmate hijacked a farmer's tractor and was apprehended doing 10 miles an hour.

As the hours fly past and the day darkens on the brook, our own thoughts must also turn to escape. Our final stop is a Slaughtered Lamb-style pub for a pint of the aptly named Dartmoor Jail Ale, drank slowly. All the folklore, the ghosts and the outlandish stories become less of a laughing matter as the sun exits, and as we follow the twisting road home, the tops of tors blacken like burnt coals. The valleys become empty pits, sheep's eyes glow in the headlights and the stars are wild and bright as we make our exit via winding lanes, back to civilisation. ●

MORE FROM **DOMINIC GARNETT**

FLYFISHING FOR COARSE FISH (MERLIN UNWIN BOOKS): The convention-busting book that became an Amazon Bestseller. Hailed as a modern classic, it details tactics, techniques, flies and novel ideas on all the major coarse species in a lively, absorbing style.

"The most original, fascinating and eye-opening fishing book I've read in years." Scottish Sun

CANAL FISHING: A PRACTICAL GUIDE (MERLIN UNWIN BOOKS): With hundreds of miles of untapped fishing, canals offer a huge range of exciting, affordable sport. This beautifully illustrated volume opens up a world of species, methods and possibilities, as well as an extensive guide to UK canal venues, including both local and national specimen fish records.

TANGLES WITH PIKE (WWW.DGFISHING.CO.UK):
From backwater England to the great lakes of Scandinavia, Tangles with Pike captures the glory of pike fishing, along with a handful of guts. Armed with just a rod, a bag of herrings and his own creaking sanity, Dominic Garnett brings you a selection of fiercely entertaining stories and articles. Spanning several years of original writing along with fresh work, this collection takes you straight to the snaggy edge of the water, where the pike are savage and the truth is as strange as the locals.

"One of the most readable angling writers in the business." Angling Times

DG FISHING

www.dgfishing.co.uk

DG FISHING: The author's site has further words, photography, and much more. Besides great books, you'll find some unique gifts, deadly flies and guided fishing days in Devon and Somerset. For further angling misadventures you can also catch the Crooked Lines blog. Take a look at: **www.dgfishing.co.uk**

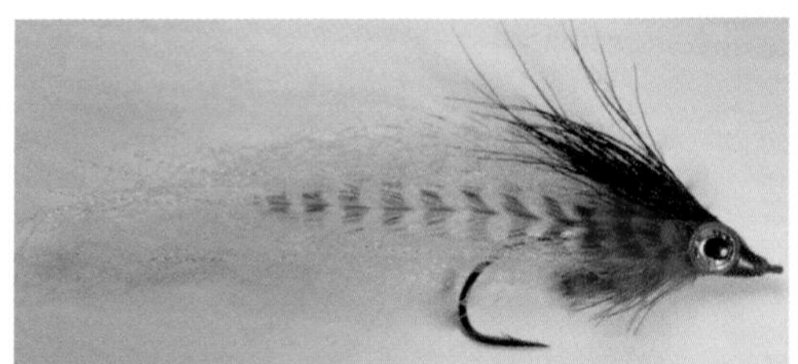

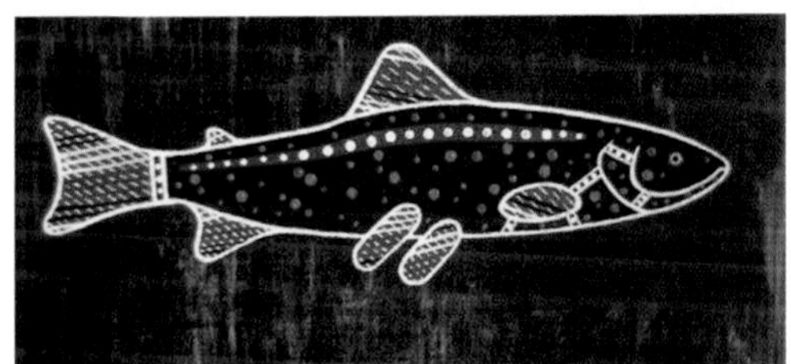

MORE FROM **DOMINIC GARNETT**

Fly For Coarse: Discover the thrill of catching coarse fish on the fly with this exciting new site and annual competition. From rudd, roach and carp, to chub, pike and even species such as barbel and zander, the possibilities are endless. The site has useful tips, fly patterns, a venue guide and a growing gallery of brilliantly varied catches from anglers all over the UK and beyond. There are some great prizes to be won each year, with a judging panel including John Bailey and Matt Hayes looking for skill, adventure and creativity, rather than simply the weight of the fish. Find out more at: **www.flyforcoarse.com**

www.dgfishing.co.uk

NOTES

NOTES

www.dgfishing.co.uk